A SHORT HANDBOOK OF LITERARY TERMS

A SHORT HANDBOOK
of LITERARY TERMS
By GEORGE G. LOANE

FOLCROFT LIBRARY EDITIONS / 1972

Limited to 150 Copies

A SHORT HANDBOOK
of LITERARY TERMS
By GEORGE G. LOANE

NEW YORK
THE MACMILLAN COMPANY

PRINTED IN GREAT BRITAIN

PREFACE

BEING once asked to recommend a book which should explain the more or less technical terms of the literary art, I was unable to find any such work extant. Yet it seemed that even the smaller points of craftsmanship were capable of being treated in such a manner as not only to benefit the student, but also to interest the large class of readers who love literature in the larger and more general way. The fact that many of these points are designated by unfamiliar, and therefore at first sight repulsive, Greek names is unfortunate but indubitable. Puttenham's valiant attempt to anglicize the terms came to nothing. We should not really gain much by calling Irony " the drie mocke " or Hyperbole " the loud liar," pleasant though the phrases be. But to know the meaning of such a word as Prolepsis, and to realize that it is of wider application in English than a casual reader might suppose, is in its small way a help rather than a hindrance to our appreciation. By no means all the terms here treated are

PREFACE

of narrow significance, and many of the 170 articles deal with matters important in the history of our literature. The alphabetical arrangement seemed most convenient, and copious cross-references have been indicated by the use of thick type in the body of the articles.

4 *Linnell Close, N.W.*11.

CONTENTS

	PAGE		PAGE
ABSTRACT FOR CONCRETE	11	CÆSURA	37
ACCENT	12	CATCH	37
ALEXANDRINE	13	CHIASMUS	38
ALLEGORY	14	CLASSICAL	39
ALLITERATION	15	CLICHÉ	40
AMBIGUITY	16	CLIMAX	41
AMPLIFICATION	18	COCKNEY SCHOOL	42
ANACOLUTHON	20	CONCEITS	43
ANAPÆST	21	CORRECTNESS	45
ANTICLIMAX	22	CORRELATIVE VERSES	46
ANTITHESIS	23	CRITICISM	47
APHORISM	25		
APOLOGUE	26	DACTYL	49
APOSIOPESIS	27	DIALECT	50
APOSTROPHE	27	DIDACTIC POETRY	51
ARCHAISM	28	DOGGEREL	52
ASSONANCE	29	DORIC	53
ATTIC	30		
AUGUSTAN	30	ELEGIAC STANZA	55
		ELEGY	55
		ELISION	56
BALLADS	32	ELLIPSE	57
BALLAD METRE	32	ENJAMBMENT	58
BATHOS	33	EPIC	59
BLANK VERSE	34	EPIGRAM	61
BOMBAST	35	EPITHETS	63
BUCOLIC	36	ESSAY	65
BURLESQUE	36	ETHIC DATIVE	67

CONTENTS

	PAGE		PAGE
EUPHEMISM	67	LITOTES	99
EUPHONY	68	LYRIC	99
EUPHUISM	69		
EXPLETIVES	70	MACARONIC VERSE	101
		MACHINERY	102
FABLE	71	MADRIGAL	103
FEMININE ENDING	72	MEIOSIS. *See* LITOTES	103
FEMININE CÆSURA	72	MASQUES	103
FIGURATIVE	72	METAPHOR	105
FIGURES OF SPEECH	73	METAPHYSICAL POETS	106
FOOT	74	METONYMY	107
FOURTEENER	75	MOCK-HEROIC	108
		MONOSYLLABLES	109
GENERAL	77	MUSE	111
GENITIVE	78		
GRUB STREET	79	NARRATIVE POETRY	113
		NOMINATIVE ABSOLUTE	114
HEMISTICH	81	NONSENSE VERSES	115
HENDIADYS	81	NOVELS	116
HEROIC (VERSE, POEM, COUPLET)	82	OCTOSYLLABICS	118
HEXAMETERS	83	ODE	119
HIATUS	85	ONOMATOPŒIA	120
HUMOUR	86	OXYMORON	123
HYPERBOLE	87		
HYSTERON PROTERON	89	PARABLE	124
		PARADOX	124
IAMB	90	PARODY	125
IDYLL	90	PARONOMASIA	125
IMPERSONAL CON-		PARTICLES	127
STRUCTION	91	PASTICHE	128
INNUENDO	91	PASTORAL POETRY	129
INVERSION	92	PATHETIC FALLACY	130
IRONY	93	PAUSE	131
		PEDANTESQUE	132
LAKE SCHOOL	96	PEGASUS	132
LEONINE VERSES	97	PENTAMETER	133
LIMERICK	98	PERIOD	133

CONTENTS

	PAGE		PAGE
PERIPHRASIS	134	SLANG	166
PERSONIFICATION	136	SOLECISM	168
PICARESQUE	137	SONNET	169
PINDARIC ODE	138	SPENSERIAN STANZA	170
PLAGIARISM	139	SPONDEE	171
PLEONASM	140	STANZA	172
POETIC LICENCE	142	STICHOMYTHIA	173
POETRY, FORMS OF	143	STYLE	174
PRECIOUS	143	SYLLEPSIS	176
PRE-RAPHAELITISM	144	SYNECDOCHE	177
PROLEPSIS	145	SYNONYMS	178
PYRRHIC	146		
		TASTE	180
QUANTITY	147	TAUTOLOGY. *See* PLEONASM	
QUATRAIN	148	TECHNICAL TERMS	181
		TERZA-RIMA. *See* STANZA	
REFRAIN	149		
REPETITION	150		
RHETORIC	152	TRANSFERRED EPITHET	182
RHYME	153	TRIBRACH	183
RHYTHM	156	TRIPLET	183
ROMANCE	158	TROCHEE	184
ROMANTIC	159		
		UNITIES	186
SARCASM	160		
SATANIC SCHOOL	160	WARDOUR-STREET ENGLISH	188
SATIRE	161		
SCANSION	162	WIT	188
SIGMATISM	164		
SIMILE	165	ZEUGMA	191

A SHORT HANDBOOK OF LITERARY TERMS

A

Abstract for Concrete.—In all languages, words which properly denote an action, state, or quality are liable to become the names of material objects. Latin examples are *fructus, civitas, legio, mansio*. We are accustomed to this in titles of honour : e.g. his majesty, your reverence, your lordship. We use " youth " for " young man." Poets carry the usage farther. Goldsmith describes the village inn as a place " where grey-beard *mirth* and smiling *toil* retired," meaning " merry old men and jolly labourers." While Thomson's green serpent lies by a stream,

> all other *thirst*, appalled,
> Or shivering flies, or checked at distance stands,
> Nor dare approach—

meaning thirsty creatures. It is characteristic of Sir Thomas Browne's highly poetical prose : e.g. " Insolent *zeals*, that do decry good works and rely only upon faith, take not away merit "—meaning zealots. It is the converse of the figure **Personification,** which treats an abstract idea as a concrete person. The prose of the eighteenth century uses it to excess; it abounds in such terms as "criticism pronounces," "good-nature will not admit," meaning critics and good-natured people.

Accent.—In every word of two or more syllables, one syllable is pronounced with special emphasis or stress, and is said to carry the accent, to be accented. The emphasis is given by a louder tone of voice, with or without a higher pitch of tone: e.g. begín, machíne, daínty, próbable, cértainly, animósity. Monosyllables in a sentence usually carry an accent, but conjunctions, prepositions, and pronouns, of one syllable, are not accented unless they are emphatic, i.e. contrasted with another of their kind expressed or understood: e.g. Wé know better. Come wíth your shield or ón it. Accent is so important an element of English speech, and consequently of English verse— "the chief lord and grave governor of numbers," Daniel calls it—that we define feet in poetry by accent, not by **quantity** as the Greeks and Romans did. The phrase "verse-accent" is sometimes used, referring to those syllables in a line on which the accent would lie if the line was normal (see **Scansion**): e.g. "The bóy|stoód *on*|the búrn|ing déck," a four-foot iambic line varied by a trochee in the second place. It is a very elementary error to accent the " on " in reading, but we probably give it a little more value than if it were the first syllable of its foot. Long words may have two accents: e.g. vúlnerabílity.

Alexandrine.—The iambic line of six accents is so named from the old French *Roman d'Alexandre* written in that metre. It is as much the standard line of French poetry as the iambic line with five accents is of English (see **Heroic**). It was introduced into English by Wyatt and Surrey, and Spenser found a splendid use for it as the closing line of his stanza. Drayton's huge *Poly-Olbion* is written entirely in Alexandrines, and the heavy metre contributes to the alleged un- readability of that—in parts charming— work. Cowley first introduced it among **heroic couplets** for variety ; Dryden so used it with freedom ; but Pope had qualms about its **correctness,** and excluded it entirely from his translation of the *Iliad*. Gray uses it to round off the majestic paragraphs of his great odes: e.g. " With necks in thunder clothed, | and long-resounding pace." Most writers have felt the necessity of this **pause** after the third accent ; Gray says that this necessity [and the resulting lack of variety] is the reason why Alexandrines are no longer used except to finish a lyric stanza ; but Dryden sometimes neglected it : e.g. " And with paternal thun|der vindicates his throne." Such apparent Alexandrines as occur occasionally in Milton's **blank verse,** e.g. " for solitude sometimes is best society," lacking the sixth accent, are best classed as extensions of the **feminine ending.** Cp. Keats's " Miltonian storms, and more, Miltonian tenderness." Browning's *Fifine at the Fair* is a modern poem in Alexandrines.

Allegory.—Coleridge defines allegory as " the employment of a set of agents and images to convey in disguise a moral meaning —those agents and images being so combined as to form a homogeneous whole." The most obvious example in English is *The Pilgrim's Progress*, which describes the adventures of the human soul under the guise of a journey. As works of literary art are the product of the writer's, and minister to the reader's, high enjoyment, and as the enjoyment of moral truths differs sharply from the enjoyment of beautiful language, beautiful sound, and imaginative truth—the saint and the artist being quite different persons—it follows that the allegory, being designed to appeal to discordant faculties of the mind, is seldom a complete success. Much of the popularity of *The Pilgrim's Progress* is due to the fact that we may forget the moral meaning, in the dramatic interest of the story. This is even more true of *The Faerie Queene*; though the dramatic interest belongs to the separate episodes rather than to the main story—which is involved and obscure—yet the imaginative and sensuous interests are so strong as almost to obliterate the moral meaning. See **Apologue, Fable, Metaphor, Parable.**

Alliteration is the close succession of words (or syllables) beginning with the same sound. It is the counterpart of **rhyme.** Such similarities naturally please us. "Even the babbling babe loves to duplicate sounds." It is common in proverbial phrases: e.g. time and tide, blessing and bane, bag and baggage, hearth and home. "Nothing takes the oriental mind so much as a retort jingling or alliterative." When Mr. Kipling was asked to write a song for the Irish Unionists, he replied: "You want drilling a damned sight more than doggerel." It is a part of the mechanism of all poetry. Tennyson said: "When I spout my lines first, they come out so alliteratively that I have sometimes no end of trouble to get rid of the alliteration;" and Swinburne undoubtedly carries the practice to excess. It forms an element of great beauty in the poems of Spenser, Milton, and Coleridge, and in the prose of Ruskin. Strangely enough it is not prominent in Keats. For perfection it must be insinuated rather than obtruded on the ear, and that is perhaps why Coleridge called alternate alliteration " a great secret in melody " : e.g. his heavy-shotted hammock-shrowd (Tennyson) : fierce noises of the fiery nightingales (Swinburne) : though frosts may blight the freshness of its bloom (Shelley). Young's clever lines—

> When fortitude has lost its fire,
> And freezes into fear—

show how alliteration helps **antithesis ;** and there is a remarkable effect of **onomatopœia** in the change from open to close vowels.

Ambiguity may come from excessive brevity ; *brevis esse laboro, obscurus fio,* says Horace. De Quincey thus analyses Pope's couplet—

> Know, God and Nature only are the same :
> In man the judgment shoots at flying game—

" The first line would naturally construe into this: that God and Nature were in harmony, whilst all other objects were scattered into incoherence by difference and disunion. Not at all ; it means nothing of the kind ; but that God and Nature only are exempted from the infirmities of change.

AMBIGUITY

They only continue uniform and self-consistent. This *might* mislead many readers; but the second line *must* do so, for who would not understand the syntax to be that the judgment, as it exists in man, shoots at flying game? But, in fact, the meaning is that the judgment, in aiming its calculations at man, aims at an object that is still on the wing, and never for a moment stationary." Words with more than one meaning require careful handling e.g., "An apparent error" may be an evident error, or an error only in appearance. The ambiguity of the word "lie" has been of much service to wits: e.g. "Sir, you lie— under a misapprehension." Praed says of the friends of his youth—

> Some lie beneath the churchyard stone,
> And some—before the Speaker.

Even the great Donne allowed himself the same quibble—

> I am unable, yonder beggar cries,
> To stand, or move; if he say true, he lies.

Wordsworth was sublimely unconscious of the ambiguity when he wrote "Heaven lies about us in our infancy." **Inversion** is a cause of ambiguity. In Gray's lines—

> The boast of heraldry, the pomp of power,
> And all that beauty, all that wealth e'er gave,
> Awaits alike th' inevitable hour—

an early editor, not seeing that "hour" is subject, printed "await," and the error is still alive. Abbot and Seeley, noticing the ambiguous use of participles, quote the passage in *Paradise Lost* where Satan first encounters Adam and Eve—

> When Adam, first of men,
> To first of women, Eve, thus moving speech,
> Turned him all ear to hear new utterance flow—

and they add that "moving" may refer to Eve or Adam, which is true enough. But the critics were themselves deceived by the ambiguity of "him," which they have noticed elsewhere. They refer it to Adam, and take "all ear" as describing Eve. This would be difficult indeed. "Him" is Satan, and Adam's preparation for a harangue made Satan prick up his ears to hear the novelty of human language—Hebrew, no doubt, though some have said Dutch.

Amplification is a necessary part of oratory, and of music. The ear as compared with the eye is a slow road to the brain; whether an idea is to be impressed or a state of feeling established, we must be given time; bare repetition is useful, but more effective is repetition with new detail, which we call amplification. Poetry being now more often read than recited, we can renew the impression as often as we please, and therefore the need of amplification is not so much recognized by poets; but still, as Dr. Henry says, the mind likes its leisure, its progress through a poem must not be a mere succession of jolts, and of objects passed by so rapidly as not to be distinguished. **Similes** are often used in this way, as in Shelley's *Skylark*. The form of the **heroic couplet** lends itself almost too readily to amplification, when a single idea has to be expanded to fill two lines. Dryden renders a sentence of Virgil—mortalia corda per gentes humilis stravit pavor—describing the effect of thunder—

> Deep horror seizes every human breast,
> Their pride is humbled, and their fear confessed.

Amplification may thus easily sink to mere dilution, and weaken the impression which it is meant to fortify. This is common in sermons, and in paraphrases of Scripture. Even Milton sins in this way, and the notorious Sir Richard Blackmore is a great criminal. Where Job says " I washed my feet in butter," his paraphrast writes—

> With teats distended with their milky store,
> Such numerous lowing herds, before my door,
> Their painful burden to unload did meet,
> That we with butter might have washed our feet.

AMPLIFICATION—ANACOLUTHON

Even a clever man like Prior could rob a famous saying of all its vigour—

> Take but the humblest lily of the field,
> And if our pride will to our reason yield,
> It must by sure comparison be shown,
> That on the regal seat great David's son,
> Arrayed in all his robes and types of power,
> Shines with less glory than that simple flower.

Swift calls amplification " the spinning-wheel of the **Bathos**." The rhetorical effectiveness of the figure is illustrated by Sir T. Browne's description of Satan's avoidance of holy water : " these are but Parthian flights, ambuscado retreats, and elusory tergiversations." Cp. Burke's censure of an imitation of Dr. Johnson's style : " it has all his pomp without his force ; it has all the nodosities of the oak without its strength " ; and then, perhaps remembering Addison's 160th *Spectator*, he added : " it has all the contortions of the Sibyl without the inspiration."

Anacoluthon has been defined as " an incoherence, a construction that does not hang together : e.g. ' he bade him to tell no one, but departing show thyself, etc.," where the reported speech suddenly turns to the direct form. Milton has a fine example of this :

> Both turned, and under open sky adored
> The God that made both sky, earth, air, and heaven,
> And starry pole. Thou also madest the night,
> Maker Omnipotent, and Thou the day.

But it is usually a result of carelessness. A careful reader feels uncomfortable in reading this sentence of Burke: " If things should give us the comparative happiness of a struggle, I shall be found, I was going to say fighting (that would be foolish) but dying by the side of Mr. Pitt," where the last phrase is written as if the earlier one was " not fighting."

Anapæst is a three-syllable foot accented on the last: e.g. colonnáde, the machíne, with a rún. A well-known example of anapæstic verse is Byron's " The Assý|rian came dówn|like a wólf|on the fóld." Trochees and pyrrhics are not possible substitutes in this metre; Byron varies it a little by an occasional initial iamb—" And there|lay the steed with his nostrils all wide"; Cowper, in *The Poplar Field* and *Alexander Selkirk*, used iamb and spondee more freely, and so made a more varied music. Those who dislike the metre ought to know that Tennyson found " an exquisite flow and evenness" in *The Poplar Field*, but they will find good critics who hold it " singsong." Blake's little poem " Ah, Sunflower, weary of time," certainly has not that fault, and Swinburne used the anapæst with most musical effect, e.g. in the " Hymn to Proserpine "—

ANAPÆST—ANTICLIMAX

> And the wonderful waters knew her, and the winds and the viewless ways,
> And the roses grew rosier, and bluer the sea-blue stream of the bays.

Shelley's *Arethusa* is a masterpiece of swift beauty, and in *Sigurd the Volsung* William Morris devised a splendid metre mainly anapæstic.

Anticlimax.—This occurs when successive statements, instead of leading to a **climax,** become less interesting or important. Unless used intentionally, for comic effect, it is a gross blunder. Waller, in praising Cromwell, wrote :

> Under the tropics is our language spoke,
> And part of Flanders hath received our yoke.

Even Pope wrote of Murray—

> Graced as thou art with all the power of words,
> Known to the Courts, the Commons, and the Lords.

to which a parodist replied—

> Persuasion tips his tongue whene'er he talks,
> And he has chambers in the King's Bench Walks.

So Pope improved his second line to—

> So known, so honoured, at the House of Lords.

Several legal anecdotes illustrate this figure, as of the judge charging a jury in a case of larceny: "For forty centuries the thunders of Sinai have echoed through the world 'Thou shalt not steal!' It is also a principle of the common law and a rule of equity." Gray uses it well in his poem about the cat and the gold-fishes—

> What female heart can gold despise?
> What cat's averse to fish?

C. S. Calverley has several amusing poems the point of which is the sudden drop from pathos in the last line. Many of the epitaphs illustrating the figure are probably as apocryphal as this on General Wolfe—

> He marched without dread or fears,
> At the head of his bold grenadiers;
> And what was remarkable—nay, very particular—
> He climbed up rocks that were perpendicular.

See **Bathos.**

Antithesis.—The nature of anything is made clearer by contrast with something else. Antithesis is the suggestion in words of such a contrast: e.g. "Man proposes, God disposes." "Men may come and men may go, But I go on for ever." It occurs in all prose and poetry, but some witty writers use it so often and so brilliantly as to give the reader an uneasy impression, as of fire-works where a steady light would be more useful. Pope, who often offends in this way, censures the practice in his satirist, Lord Hervey—

> His wit all see-saw, between *that* and *this*,
> Now high, now low, now master up, now miss,
> And he himself one vile antithesis.

Wordsworth condemns the over-intellectual, half-mechanical character of such writing; but even he once relieved himself in an " antithetic character " of Robert Jones: e.g.

> There's thought and no-thought, and there's paleness and bloom,
> And bustle and sluggishness, pleasure and gloom.

A common form of antithesis is the Balanced Sentence, in which the different clauses of a compound sentence are made similar in form: e.g. " these he could neither reject with credit nor receive with comfort." Dr. Johnson is famous for this sort of writing: e.g. " Contempt is the proper punishment of affectation, and detestation is the just consequence of hypocrisy." It occurs quite early in our language, as this word-for-word version of a passage in *The Anglo-Saxon Chronicle* shows: " Men murdered him, but God exalted him. He was in life [an] earthly king: he is now after death [a] heavenly saint." And with the addition of **chiasmus**:

"They that would not erst to his living body bend them, these now humbly on [their] knees bow to his dead bones." When a contrast can be conveyed by repeating nearly the same words, it is very effective: e.g. "this is true but not new, that is new but not true: a juggler is a wit in things, and a wit is a juggler in words: this man I thought had been a lord among wits, but I find he is only a wit among lords."

Aphorism (or apophthegm) is "the compression of a mass of thought and observation into a single saying . . . its distinction is not so much ingenuity, as good sense brought to a point. . . . It conveys some portion of a truth with such point as to set us thinking on what remains" (Lord Morley). It differs from a proverb much as a lyric poem differs from a popular ballad, being definitely the product of a single trained mind; and from a maxim, as stating a truth generally, not giving a rule of conduct. The best aphorisms are those founded on their maker's own experience; they must impress us with their wisdom rather than their cleverness. Mr. Birrell objects to Disraeli's on this ground. "The words of a true aphorism," he says, "have veins filled with the life of their utterer." The truth conveyed by aphorisms is not systematic; but, as Mill tells us, "truths each resting on its own independent evidence are none the less truths ; it is for philosophy afterwards to trace their connection." Or as Bacon, who himself made a collection of such sayings, puts it : " Knowledge, while it is in aphorisms and observations, is in growth." An aphorism, if it lacks point, is a commonplace. " Pope was probably unequalled in his power of coining aphorisms out of commonplaces" (Stephen). Walton tells us that Sir Henry Wotton, when visiting schools, would never leave without dropping some choice Greek or Latin apophthegm or sentence. In his earlier days he had got into a bad scrape by making this original aphorism on an ambassador—" an honest man sent to lie abroad for his country."

Apologue means much the same as **Fable,** but seems to be used with special reference to the instruction conveyed, and nowadays often has oriental associations. Jotham's parable (*Judges* ix. 7) is a good example. So is the tale of the Belly and the Members in early Roman History. During one of the Turkish invasions, a Pacha thus urged the reduction of the Hungarian fortresses before attacking Vienna : " A king once placed a heap of gold on the middle of a carpet, and offered it to anyone who could take it up without treading on the carpet. A wise man rolled up the carpet from a corner, and thus obtained possession of the gold. Hungary is the carpet, and if rolled up in like manner the gold may be reached in the autumn, or at the latest next spring." Macaulay uses the apologue rather savagely at the beginning of his essay on Robert Montgomery. Parnell's *The Hermit* is an eastern apologue in verse.

Aposiopesis is an abrupt stoppage, the sentence being left incomplete for the sake of effect: e.g. "And if it bear fruit—but if not, cut it down." The figure is very effective in threats. Virgil's *quos ego*—is the most famous example in literature, and we hear such expressions as "If you don't drop that, I'll—— " In the fifteenth century two paper-saving Irish chieftains are said to have exchanged the following correspondence: "Pay me tribute, or else—— " "I owe you none, and if—— " The "Hymn to Pan" in Keats's *Endymion* has an example—

> Be still a symbol of immensity;
> A firmament reflected in a sea;
> An element filling the space between;
> An unknown—— but no more: we humbly screen
> With uplift hands our foreheads, lowly bending. . . .

Apostrophe.—" This consists in addressing something absent, as if present; as when an orator invokes some hero of other times, or a preacher appeals to angels and departed saints. It supposes great intensity of emotion" (Bain). E.g. "O Jerusalem, Jerusalem! thou that killest the prophets!" "O death, where is thy sting?" At the beginning of the third book of *Paradise Lost* Milton magnificently apostrophizes light: "Hail! holy light, offspring of Heaven first-born." Wordsworth uses the figure finely: "Milton! thou shouldst be living at this hour." Like all such forms of speech, it becomes ridiculous when the emotion is not sincere, as in the poem on vaccination beginning "Inoculation! heavenly maid, descend!" where the improbability of the **Personification** adds a further element of absurdity. Of the same sort are those countless invocations of a **Muse** which impress us as being addressed to a being reluctant, if at all existent. Hence apostrophe is a common device of the humorist or the satirist. "It is a liberty taken with exalted objects and persons to address them with familiarity, and the result is degrading and thence ludicrous. The writings of Carlyle abound with this employment of the figure" (Bain).

Archaism is the deliberate use of obsolete words or syntax. Spenser, seemingly in imitation of Theocritus's **Doric,** wrote thus in his *Shepheard's Calender,* for which he is pleasantly defended by E. K. in the Preface : " In whom [the poets] whenas this our Poet hath bene much traveiled and thoroughly redd, how could it be (as that worthy oratour sayde) but that walking in the sonne, although for other cause he walked, yet needes he mought be sunburnt, and, having the sound of those ancient Poets still ringing in his eares, he mought needes, in singing, hit out some of theyr tunes." Dryden says with his usual good sense : " When an ancient word for its sound and significancy deserves to be revived, I have that reasonable veneration for antiquity to restore it. All beyond this is superstition." Archaism will be unsuccessful when the old words do not seem to belong naturally to the writer's style, but appear to be dragged in, and savour of affectation. Such writing has been called **Wardour Street English.** Opinions will differ as to the success of such efforts, as in the case of Butcher and Lang's translation of Homer. There can be no doubt of the irritating effect of such expressions as " understanded of the people," " yclept " and the like in modern journalism.

Assonance is an imperfect (and often earlier) form of **rhyme.** It requires the last accented vowel sounds of lines—and succeeding vowels, if any—to be identical ; whereas rhyme requires, as well as this, the identity of succeeding consonants. Fate, take ; glory, holy ; make assonance but not rhyme.

Attic.—Attica being the region of which Athens was chief town, and Athens " the eye of Greece " being the home of nearly all the most polished Greek writers, the word " Attic " is used to describe a style at once simple, pure and elegant, such as Addison's. " Salt " is a Latinism for " wit," therefore Attic salt is refined wit. Pope ascribed Attic wit to Lord Chesterfield. In Sterne's novel Mr. Shandy, having brought off a witty retort to an offending servant, was thus affected : " Triumph swam in my father's eyes at the repartee ; the Attic salt brought tears into them ;—and so Obadiah heard no more about it."

Augustan.—The reign of Augustus is known as the golden age of Latin literature, the period when letters and learning arrived at their highest perfection. This combination of letters and learning is an important part of the conception of an Augustan Age. There is nothing Augustan about Shakespeare or Burns. The age of Pope Leo X. in Italy, and that of Louis XIV in France, have been given the same title, and Goldsmith first claimed it for the reign of Queen Anne, or some years before that period, in England. As Virgil, Horace, Ovid, and Livy set a standard of style for Rome, so Shaftesbury, Swift, Pope, Bolingbroke, Addison, and Steele were conceived to have done for England. It is remarkable that Goldsmith names only prose writers. He himself introduced a more natural style of poetry than that produced by Pope and his followers, of which he seems to have felt the inadequacy. The reaction was carried further by Cowper, Burns, and Blake, and culminated in the publication by Wordsworth and Coleridge of *Lyrical Ballads* in 1798. See **Lake School, Romantic.**

B

Ballads are traditional songs, of unknown authorship, transmitted by the people. They have their origin in a popular choral drama, the chief characters singing their parts, and the chorus contributing a **refrain.** All the best English ballads hail from the country between the Forth and the Tyne, and date from 1350 to 1550. *Sir Patrick Spens* is a fine example, and many more will be found in Percy's *Reliques of Ancient Poetry* and similar collections. An article in Sir A. Quiller-Couch's *Studies in Literature* is illuminating. Literary imitation of the old forms has produced such fine poems as Campbell's *Lord Ullin's Daughter*, Scott's *Rosabelle* and Rossetti's *Sister Helen* ; those of his own day Dr. Johnson always ridiculed.

Ballad Metre.—Alternate lines of four and three iambic feet are so called : e.g. *John Gilpin*. The metre is the old **fourteener** broken into two parts for convenience in printing ; but sometimes the first and third lines rhyme as well as the second and fourth. Johnson held this " the most soft and pleasing of our lyric measures." But his parody is not very sympathetic:

> The tender infant, meek and mild,
>   Fell down upon the stone;
> The nurse took up the squealing child,
>   But still the child squeal'd on.

Bathos.—This is a sudden descent from the sublime, in description. Coleridge, when viewing a fine waterfall, heard a spectator describe it as "majestic," and thanked him warmly for supplying the right word. "Yes," said the flattered tourist, "it is very pretty, isn't it?" Sylvester ends a description of a thunderstorm by a comparison to striking a light with a flint and steel. Dryden, in praise of Lord Sheffield's translation of Ovid, has:

> How will sweet Ovid's ghost be pleased to hear
> His fame augmented by a British peer!

The term was first used by Pope, as the antithesis of the Greek *hypsos*, height, sublimity; bathos means depth, but was never used by the Greeks in this literary sense. Here is one of Pope's examples, of a warhorse:

> His eye-balls burn, he wounds the smoking plain,
> And knots of scarlet ribbon deck his mane.

Bentley held that Milton's description of

the rebel angels, " god-like shapes, and forms excelling human," was a bathos. But it may be considered as a very magnificent compliment to " the human face divine," another phrase of Milton's. Like **anticlimax**, bathos may be used intentionally for comic effect : e.g.

> Nightingales murmured still their loves and pities,
> And jack-asses commenced their amorous ditties.

Blank verse is verse without rhyme. We use the phrase for standard English lines of five unrhymed iambic feet, introduced by Surrey, almost perfected by Marlowe, used with final mastery by Shakespeare. After him the blank verse of drama contains so many feminine endings, and even two-syllable endings, that in Massinger and Jonson it often reads more as rhythmical prose. The standard of epic blank verse was set once for all by Milton ; its chief beauties are sonority, and variety of pause. The eighteenth-century writers depreciated the metre ; many of their attempts to write it are painful reading ; the best specimens, such as parts of Thomson and Cowper, are but lifeless imitations of Milton ; but in the colloquial manner Cowper is very happy. Wordsworth's best is very splendid, as in the *Lines Written near Tintern Abbey*, but he often writes so tamely that we get little pleasure from the metre. There is no metre which can be so easily written without distinction, so like is it to the ordinary cadence of prose. It is amusing to collect examples from prose writers. Goldsmith begins an essay, " Where Tauris lifts its head above the storm." Dickens in his pathetic passages is full of blank verse. So is Ruskin. Here is one from George Meredith: "She had outwept the colour of her eyes." And Mrs. Humphry Ward thus ends her record of Henry James : " ' There is none like him—none.' The honied lips are silent, and the helping hand at rest."

Bombast is unsuccessful **hyperbole,** the false sublime, an attempt at grandeur which does not " come off." We feel that the rider is spurring a reluctant **Pegasus,** and we resent the deliberate attack upon our admiration. As with many faults in writing, insincerity is usually the cause of the failure. When the writer is really moved, he more easily carries us with him ; but readers incapable of strong emotion are apt to find bombast where it is not. Pope gives some excellent examples from Sir Richard Blackmore ; e.g. this of a bull-baiting :

>Up to the stars the sprawling mastiffs fly,
>And add new monsters to the frighted sky.

But when Macbeth imagines his bloody

BOMBAST—BUCOLIC—BURLESQUE

hands turning the green ocean red, the murderer's agony of mind justifies the hyperbole. Burke's description of bombast is "when words commonly sacred to great occasions are put together without any rational view, or in such a manner that they do not rightly agree with each other," which sounds as if it was a mere affair of words; but of course Burke meant the ideas expressed by the words.

Bucolic means connected with herdsmen or shepherds. Virgil's **pastoral** poems are known as Bucolics, dealing as they do with country life. Pope addressed Gay as "divine bucoliast," referring to Gay's pastorals. See **Idyll.**

Burlesque differs from **mock-heroic** as the ludicrous treatment of a serious subject differs from the pompous treatment of things trivial. Gray's poem about the cat and the gold-fishes is mock-heroic. *Don Quixote* was written as a burlesque of knight-errantry. In former days, a pantomime named Robinson Crusoe would be a burlesque of that serious tale Such a poem as *The Rape of the Lock* is mock-heroic from one point of view, but it also burlesques the methods of epic poetry. *Hudibras* is a burlesque of the Puritans.

C

Cæsura in classical verse is the division of a **foot** between two words; but writers on English prosody use it for the pause which occurs naturally about the middle of a line of any length. Puttenham (1589) says that in a verse of twelve syllables (**Alexandrine**) the cæsura " ought to fall right upon [i.e. after] the sixth syllable." Surrey, the originator of **blank verse,** regularly makes a cæsura after the second accent of his five-foot iambic lines, but Spenser asserted that free placing of the pause which is one of the secrets of Milton's various harmony : e.g.

> And over them Death his triumphant dart
> Shook.

Shelley and Swinburne also use this exceptional pause after the first syllable of a line with great effect. But long passages ought to be studied to realize the manifold varieties of the pause in different writers.

Catch, equivalent to the Greek word *anacrusis*, is used for the extra unaccented syllable at the beginning of a line, when the normal line has an accent on the first syllable.

It is common in the early English accentual poetry; e.g. *Piers Plowman*. In Gray's stanza—

> Néw-born flocks, in rustic dance,
> Frísking ply their feeble feet;
> Forgétful of their wintry trance,
> The birds his presence greet—

Mr. Gosse notices the catch in the third line as "perhaps the most delicate metrical effect Gray ever attained."

Chiasmus is a cross order of two pairs of words or phrases, writing A B b a for the more ordinary A B a b: e.g. "I cannot dig, to beg I am ashamed." Gildersleeve says it is "as natural to the Greek as mother's milk; not so to us." "The body's rest, the quiet of the heart" (Sackville): "Love without end, and without measure grace" (Milton): "In shape an angel, and a god in speech" (Fairfax): "Her coat white satin, quilted; blue satin her shoes" (Richardson): "Our noblest senses act by pairs, two eyes to see, to hear, two ears" (Butler): "See Pan with flocks, with fruits Pomona crowned" (Pope): "The horse of knowledge and the learned pig" (Wordsworth): "The waves generously rise and dash angrily" (Thoreau): "It [French poetry] has sacrificed truth to perfection, and to reason life" (*Times Literary Supplement*).

Classical as opposed to **romantic** describes the pre-eminent qualities of the great Greek and Latin writers, whether found in their works or elsewhere. "The classical ideal is predominantly an intellectual one. Its products are characterized by clearness of thought, by completeness and symmetry, by harmonious proportion, by simplicity and repose. Classical works . . . are positive, clear, finished" (quoted by *N.E.D.*). It would be quite wrong to suppose that there are no romantic elements in the great Greek and Latin writers, but the qualities mentioned are so characteristic of them that the term "classical" is unobjectionable, if we realize that all the great writers include both elements though in varying proportions. Closely connected with the distinction in question is the controversy as to the personal or impersonal character of works of art. The romantic critic finds the works interesting as the revelation of a personality: the classical critic glories in the contemplation of absolute perfection untainted by any trace of human authorship. George Wyndham on the other hand held that the fundamental contrast is not between romantic and classic, but between romantic and realist. Either or both of these might become a classic by choosing, and polishing his imagination, in the first case, or his observation in the second, until the element of wonder disappeared from his image of life.

Cliché is properly a stereotype block. It is also used for a stereotyped or stock phrase, which has lost its sharpness of impression from constant and unskilful use: e.g. few and far between: ever and anon: it is a far cry to: steeped to the lips in: it stands to reason—which last has been properly described as mere bluff. Landor objected to " palmy days," and " at the eleventh hour." Jane Austen wrote to a literary niece: " I wish you would not let him ' plunge into a vortex of dissipation.' I do not object to the thing, but I cannot bear the expression; it is such thorough novel slang; and so old that I dare say Adam met with it in the first novel he opened." Leigh Hunt observes that Addison's *Cato* is full of such phrases: " plant daggers in my heart—ripe for a revolt—towers above her sex—courting the yoke—straining every nerve." Their use has been defended as being a sort of intellectual shorthand, which helps the writer, as habits save time in our actions. But good writers, valuing the expressiveness of every word, refuse such indulgences. Regarding phrases as the clothing of thoughts, they have a sentiment opposed to ready-made ones. They demand from the reader that habit of " reading with an eager mind" which Professor Bradley recommends, and which is a valuable and delightful possession, attainable by everybody. Stock phrases are mere soporifics.

Climax is the arranging of the particulars of a **period,** or other portion of discourse, so as to rise in strength to the last. The common example of this figure is from the Oration of Cicero against Verres. The orator, wishing to raise the indignation of his audience to the highest pitch, refrained from specifying the crime of the accused at once, and led the way to it by successive steps : " It is an outrage to *bind* a Roman citizen ; to *scourge* him is an atrocious crime ; to *put him to death* is almost parricide ; but to CRUCIFY him—what shall I call it ? " (Bain). A simpler specimen is this of Sidney : " My promise given, and given to Zelmane, and to Zelmane dying, prevailed more with me than my friendship to Musidorus." Dr. Johnson, in talking of his *Dictionary*, said : " I knew very well what I was undertaking, and very well how to do it, and have done it very well." We can well imagine the rising triumph of the speaker's tone. There is an admirable climax, helped by cunning alliteration, in Gilbert's *Mikado* :

To sit in solemn silence in a dull, dark dock,
In a pestilential prison with a life-long lock,
Awaiting the sensation of a short, sharp shock,
From a cheap and chippy chopper on a big, black block.

COCKNEY SCHOOL

Cockney School was a nickname fastened by *Blackwood's Magazine*, in its most scurrilous days, on Leigh Hunt, Hazlitt, Keats, and their friends; to whom Shelley was later added, perhaps on the ground of one unfortunate rhyme—name, time. No one denies that there are faults of taste and diction in Leigh Hunt, or that Keats's early verses were disfigured by some dreadful phrases and rhymes: e.g. grass, farce; parsons, fastens; wakened, spike-end. But the interest of the name is now purely antiquarian; the savagery and futility of the attack is a terrible warning to critics. Just hear Lockhart, an able man, whom his few friends loved: " They are by far the vilest vermin that ever dared to creep upon the hem of the majestic garment of the English muse. They have not one idea that is worthy of the name of English in the whole circle of their minds. . . . And yet with what an ineffable air of satisfaction these fellows speak of themselves as likely to go down to posterity among the great authors of England! It is almost a pity to destroy so excellent a joke. Unless the salt of the nickname they have got preserve them, they cannot possibly last twenty years in the recollection even of the Cockneys." Some **Cockney rhymes** have been mentioned above. Lamb objected to abroad, lord: and Tennyson corrected Eudora, before her; and vista, sister; in Jean Ingelow. But the disregard of the r sound by Southern Englishmen appears in Crabbe—cards, charades; and in Swinburne and Arnold—morning, dawning. Dr. Watts has north, wrath; and Quarles belie her, admire her.

Conceits are far-fetched, over-ingenious thoughts, very often comparisons. They are a product of the intellect, and their ingenuity may give a certain pleasure; but so far as they are not due to emotion in the writer, they fail to move ours. Quarles says that Christ's human nature is an umbrella to His divinity. He compares himself to a ship tossed on the world's sea by the winds of lusts, but he turns a good simile into an absurdity by going on:

> Repentance is the bucket, and mine eye
> The pump unused (but in extremes), and dry.

Some early poems of Dryden are full of conceit, especially that on a young nobleman who died of small-pox: e.g.

> Each little pimple had a tear in it,
> To wail the fault its rising did commit.

But his robust common sense soon asserted itself, and his mature view is expressed in the saying—" passions are serious things, and will admit no playing." But that is not the whole story. "Though there are cold conceits," says Hartley Coleridge, "all conceits are not cold. The mind, in certain states of passion, finds comfort in playing with occult or casual resemblances, and dallies with the echo of a sound." Passion may even speak in puns. "Old Gaunt indeed, and gaunt in being old," says Shakespeare's John of Lancaster, and the pun points the bitterness of his soul. Wordsworth admits that such mean instruments are made mighty when wielded by an afflicted soul, and strangeness is then the order of nature. He contrasts this conceit—

> The dews of the morning most carefully shun,
> They are tears of the sky for the loss of the sun

with Milton's splendid lines :

> Sky lowered, and, muttering thunder, some sad drops
> Wept, at completing of the mortal sin.

If this is a conceit, its sincerity is saved by the intensity of the writer's emotion ; we should never dream of calling it ingenious. So Macaulay says that Chatham's ardour and noble bearing " put fire into the most frigid conceit, and gave dignity to the most puerile allusion." It is obviously easier for an orator to do this than a poet, for his attack upon our emotions is much more direct; and many of us are void of real passion, and, "feeling nothing intensely, can intensify nothing." (Leigh Hunt).

Correctness was the literary ideal of Pope and his contemporaries. Young thus addresses him in verse:

> Excuse no fault; though beautiful, 'twill harm;
> One fault shocks more than twenty beauties charm.
> Our age demands correctness; Addison
> And you this commendable hurt have done.
> Now writers find, as once Achilles found,
> The whole is mortal, if a part's unsound.

Leslie Stephen interprets the word to mean "the quality which is gained by incessant labour, guided by quick feeling, and always under the strict supervision of common sense." If we except Milton, who dwells apart, from whatever aspect we view him, Pope was the first conscientious workman among English poets; he always took pains to write his best. His quick feeling ensured that sort of tact which distinguishes an artist in words. Common sense banished alike the great hyperboles of the Elizabethans and the quaint conceits of the Caroline poets. If the ideal was not very lofty, it at least suggests an engaging modesty—Pope never doubted the superiority of Shakespeare—and was of service in the development of the English language. Slovenly work has ever since been considered discreditable. Macaulay, in his essay on Moore's *Life of Byron*, understanding "correctness" as the observance of a number of arbitrary rules, has no difficulty in showing the absurdity of such an ideal; he "lets fly" for several pages in his most exhilarating manner. And indeed there was quite enough bad criticism in the eighteenth century to justify his wrath.

Correlative Verses are a form of abbreviated sentence, best understood by an example. Wither thus ends an epitaph:

> The poor, the world, the heavens, and the grave,
> Her alms, her praise, her soul, her body have—

meaning "the poor have her alms, the world has her praise," and so on.

So Spenser writes:

> Faint, weary, sore, emboilèd, grievèd, brent,
> With heat, toil, wounds, arms, smart, and inward fire—

And even Milton

>   Air, water, earth,
> By fowl, fish, beast, was flown, was swum, was walked.

Raleigh has a terrible example extending to twelve lines. Whether Cicero was the original sinner I know not, but here is an effort of his:

> Defendi, tenui, vetui; face, cæde, timore:
> Civis, dux, consul: tecta, lares, Latium—

i.e. Civis defendi tecta face—and so on.

In that rich storehouse of love and arms, noble eloquence and poetic artifice—Sidney's *Arcadia*—Philoclea laments the supposed perfidy of Pyrocles in a sonnet entirely composed of these lines, the sense being helped out by figures placed over the words. The last two lines will be a sufficient example:

>   1   2   3   1   2   3
> For nothing, time, nor place, can loose, quench, ease,
>   1   2   3   1   2   3
> Mine owne, embraced, sought, knot, fire, disease.

Criticism in its largest sense is the investigation, by a writer of trained intelligence and fine sensibility, of the principles which inform great works of art. Aristotle is the father of all such. Its use is to open our eyes to beauties which might escape us, and to supply an intellectual basis for the emotions which such works arouse. Incidentally, it will provide reasons for disliking what is artistically bad. Its danger is this: that the human soul is greater than any body of principles which the critic may be able to deduce

CRITICISM

whereas the principles, when once formulated, come to be considered all-sufficient. This accounts for the hopeless failure which criticism often exhibits when it has to deal with truly original works. The ordinary use of the word is to describe a judgment on an individual literary work or writer. The best criticism is that which helps us to sympathetic reflexion on the work in question; hence even the critic who only conveys to us his own enjoyment, without giving good reasons for it—like Leigh Hunt—is of use; indeed Professor Dowden says that the best criticism of Shakespeare is of this kind. Some of the best English critics are Coleridge, Lamb, Pater, and Matthew Arnold. Leslie Stephen says that " in some sense all criticism is a nuisance and a parasite growth upon literature," but his own *Hours in a Library* shows clearly that this is not the whole truth.

D

Dactyl is a **foot** consisting of one accented syllable followed by two unaccented: e.g. beáutiful, cóme to me, stréngthen us. A familiar example of dactylic metre is the hymn—" Brightest and best of the sons of the morning." Poe has a specimen of pure dactyls:

> Can it be fancied that Deity ever vindictively
> Made in his image a mannikin merely to madden it?

Lamb is not very kind to some early dactyls of Southey; he was moved to parody a rhythm which evidently did not please his ear—

> Sorely your dactyls do drag along limp-footed . . .
> Dismal your dactyls are, God help ye, rhyming ones!

But Hood used them successfully in his famous *The Bridge of Sighs*; and Dryden has a charming song beginning—

> After the pangs of a desperate lover,
>   When night and day I have sighed all in vain,
> Ah what a pleasure it is to discover
>   In her eyes pity, who causes my pain!

Browning's *The Lost Leader* has fine lines: e.g.

> We that had loved him so, followed him, honoured him,
> Lived in his mild and magnificent eye.

Tennyson's *Charge of the Light Brigade* is a less happy example; such a line as

> " While horse and héro fell "

would hardly have pleased Lamb. See **Hexameter.**

Dialect is a special local form of a language e.g. that of the Scots Lowlands, which is a dialect of English. Burns is the most obvious instance of a great writer whose best work is not done in the standard literary language; but it must be remembered that his dialect has a literary tradition reaching back to the days of Chaucer. William Barnes wrote poems in the dialect of Dorsetshire. Tennyson's *Northern Farmer* is a good example. The short prose tales of Bret Harte owe some of their charm to the unfamiliar language of the western American. Mr. Kipling has made much use of dialect in his short stories and *Barrack-room Ballads,* and George Eliot's tales of provincial life naturally introduce it in dialogue. The literary advantage of dialect is that its strange forms and idioms fix our attention; they have not been dulled to our mental ear by constant use; the "veil of familiarity"—to use Shelley's fine phrase—does not obscure their illuminating power. On the other hand, if the dialect is too difficult, the reader's natural laziness is apt to assert itself. At the end of the last century the term " Kailyard School " was used to describe certain popular writers of Scottish fiction in dialect. One of them was " Ian Maclaren," whose *Beside the Bonnie Briar Bush* owed its title to a Jacobite song, " There grows a bonnie briar bush in our kail yard " (*N.E.D.*).

Didactic Poetry professes to instruct us in the subject of which it treats. If it does that by quickening our sympathies and stimulating our imagination it may still be good poetry, as well as instructive; but poetry gains nothing by such " an unstable combination of discordant elements." Instruction is properly conveyed in prose. Didactic poems may rely mainly on argument or on description. Lucretius's *De Rerum Natura*, setting out the philosophy of Epicurus, is full of argument of the driest kind, along with descriptions of great brilliance or pathos. Other poems of this class, though far inferior in poetic power, are Dryden's *Religio Laici* and *The Hind and the Panther*, exhibiting respectively the Anglican and the Roman Catholic forms of religion; and Pope's *Essay*

DIDACTIC POETRY—DOGGEREL

on Man, a versification of Bolingbroke's views. Of the descriptive class the finest is again Roman—Virgil's *Georgics,* on farming; Phillips's *Cyder,* Dyer's *Fleece,* and Darwin's *Botanic Garden* are now mere names; but Pope's brilliant *Essay on Criticism* is not likely ever to be quite forgotten. The best parts of such poems are the least didactic; the poet seizes greedily any opportunity of picturesque description or appeal to our moral feeling. Not even the ardour of Lucretius's missionary spirit can blind us to the aridity of large tracts of his wonderful poem. Still less can Darwin's amazing cleverness induce us to forget his inhuman heartlessness. " His volcanic head flamed with imagination [i.e. fancy], but his torpid heart slept unawakened by passion " (D'Israeli).

Doggerel is a rather vague term of abuse, applied to inartistic verse with close-recurring rhymes, strong and monotonous rhythm, and a general lack of dignity. Chaucer used it for " undistinguished or unpoetic verse or rhyme of any kind." Puttenham says that in doggerel " the over busy and too speedy return of one manner of tune doth too much annoy and as it were glut the ear, unless it be in small and popular musicks sung by these Cantabanqui upon benches and barrels' heads, or else by blind harpers or such like tavern minstrels that give a fit of mirth for a groat, and their matters being for the most part stories of old time, as the tale of *Sir Topas*, the reports of *Bevis of Southampton*, and *Guy of Warwick*." He goes on to include the rhymes of Skelton, but Skelton's immense vivacity and virulence give his doggerel a unique interest ; and he can do better than doggerel at times. He thus describes the pompous houses of the clergy—

> Building royally
> Their mansions curiously
> With turrets and with towers,
> With halls and with bowers,
> Stretching to the stars ;
> With glass windows and bars,
> Hanging about the walls
> Cloths of gold and palls ;
> Arras of rich array,
> Fresh as flowers in May—

and so on. Well might Bishop Hall characterize such stuff as " Angry Skelton's breathless rhymes." More modern writers, as Ruskin and Thackeray, have liked to play as Swift did with doggerel in their lighter moments.

Doric.—As the first **pastoral** poets, Theocritus, Bion and Moschus, wrote in the Doric dialect of Greek, Milton in *Lycidas* uses " Doric lay " for pastoral poem. Doric not being the principal literary form of Greek, " Doric " has come to be used of any local

DORIC

variation from the standard form of a language, even of an Irish brogue. See **Dialect.** Further, though there is nothing rustic about Theocritus except his subject, " Doric " may now be applied to rustic speech generally, and even to rustic manners. Spenser introduced homely and provincial words in his *Shepheard's Calender*, an innovation of which Sidney did not approve.

E

Elegiac Stanza.—The four-lined stanza of heroic lines rhyming alternately, used in Gray's *Elegy*, has been so named; though it was used by Davenant in his heroic poem *Gondibert*, and by Dryden in *Annus Mirabilis*, a poem of historical description. Sir John Davies's *Nosce Teipsum* is a philosophic poem in this stanza.

Elegy is (1) a song of lamentation over someone dead; (2) a personal, reflective poem, its principal themes being sorrow and love. The great English elegies of the first sort are Milton's *Lycidas*, Tennyson's *In Memoriam*—a series of poems in memory of Arthur Hallam—and Matthew Arnold's *Thyrsis*, on Clough. The least suspicion of insincerity damns an elegy, and we feel with Cleveland—

> I like not tears in tune, nor do I prize
> His artificial grief who scans his eyes.

Gray's famous *Elegy in a Country Churchyard* is of the second class, and of miscellaneous elegies Shenstone supplies a fine assortment, on such various subjects as Ophelia's urn, the turbulence of love compared with the tranquillity of friendship, to a lady on the language of birds, a vision of Wolsey's ghost, his disinterestedness, lamentation on the state of the woollen manufactory, his subjection to Delia, body-snatching—all extremely pensive, and strongly sounding the personal note.

Elision.—When a word ends in a vowel, and the following word begins with one, the first vowel is often dropped out of the metre, or made to coalesce with the following one. This was the regular practice of Greek and Latin poets, and adds a nameless charm (e.g.) to Virgil's versification; notice his splendid phrase—*strepitumque Acheruntis avari*. Milton's use of elision is worth study; Cowper held that it gave great majesty to his verse. Here is the famous opening of *Paradise Lost* iii, the elisions marked by inverted commas in the manner introduced by Bentley:

> Hail, holy Light, offspring of Heaven first-born!
> Or of the' Eternal coëternal beam
> May I express thee' unblamed.

Elision may also occur within a word, as in the trisyllabic scansion of such a word as "impetuous." Opinion has differed sharply as to the treatment of elision in reading. Some try to exclude it, by pronouncing a three-syllable foot. The eighteenth century, on the contrary, committed to the ten-syllable theory of heroic lines, insisted on dropping the first vowel altogether, and on printing (e.g.) " wat'ry " for " watery." But that seems to us very ugly, and is clearly impossible in such a line as Milton's " Virtue' in her shape how lovely; saw and pined." Even Erasmus Darwin says that anyone's ear will readily determine there is no elision in " And vocal rose-buds thrill the enchanted grove." There is something additional to the normal syllabic metre, but not quite as much as a syllable. When the metre shows that the first vowel is not to be elided, it is said to be " open." Pope knew that open vowels (see **Hiatus**) tire the ear, and Swinburne says that " elision is a necessity, not a luxury, of metre." It contributes to that variety at which the poet is always aiming, without entirely obliterating the normal form of the line.

Ellipse is the omission, for the sake of brevity, of words required to make full sense. It is quite common in ordinary speech : e.g. " season " for " season ticket " ; and in recognised phrases, as " a coach and six," " St. Paul's," " the Channel " for " the English Channel." " Cessation " is the earlier equivalent of " armistice." The single word " impossible ! " is far more effective than a complete sentence. Pope uses the figure to excess : e.g. " Man never is, but always to be, blest," for " man never is blest, but always about to be blest " ; and cp.

Heaven from all creatures hides the book of fate,
All but the page prescribed, their present state ;
From brutes what men, from men what spirits know—

where the last line perhaps carries brevity too far. Ellipse is bad if the words to be supplied are not used elsewhere : e.g. " I neither have, nor ever will, love parsing." The common ellipse of the relative pronoun is a frequent cause of obscurity in English : e.g. " O that forc'd thunder [that] from his breath did fly."

Enjambment means running the sentence past the end of an **heroic couplet,** in contrast with the method of Waller and Pope, who nearly always closed it there. Daniel, writing in 1607, found it " rather graceful than otherwise." Little more than a hundred years later Prior, in the preface to *Solomon*, holding enjambment as practised by Donne " too dissolute and wild, and very often coming too near prose," condemned equally the end-stopped couplet, corrected by Davenant and Waller, and perfected by Dryden, as " bringing every couplet to the point of an epigram." His own compromise did not avail to vitalize his epic. Seven years earlier Pope had produced his *Essay on Criticism*, but Prior could hardly have foreseen the tyranny which Pope's masterly technique was to impose on English verse for nearly a hundred years. The reaction was bound to come. Already in 1774 we find Gilbert White, the naturalist, advising his nephew to vary his cadences, i.e. the positions of the **pause,** and to " throw the sense and pause into the third line, which adds a dignity and freedom to your expressions." The **Romantic** poets threw Pope completely overboard, and Keats in *Endymion* and better still in *Lamia* restored freedom of movement to the couplet, and full liberty of enjambment.

Epic is usually held synonymous with **heroic poem.** Homer's *Iliad* and *Odyssey* have set a standard to all succeeding poets, and from them also Aristotle drew the famous " rules " over which the critics have quarrelled much. It seems essential to the idea of an epic (1) that its action should be one, great, and entire ; (2) that its hero should be distinguished, and move our concern ; (3) that the episodes should easily arise from the main fable, i.e. there should be no parts detachable without loss to the whole. Wordsworth and Coleridge agreed with the earlier critics that the agency of beings superior to man (see **Machinery**) is a necessary part of the conception. Length is clearly essential. To succeed in such a poem requires a comprehensive intellect of the first order, and great industry, in addition to the sensibility which is characteristic of all poets. Hence the scarcity of great epics. Virgil's *Æneid*, Dante's *Divine Comedy*, Tasso's *Jerusalem Delivered*, Milton's *Paradise Lost*—these are usually admitted to the first class. Spenser's *Faerie Queene* was never completed, but it is improbable that its rambling **fable** could have been unified by any additions. It seems that the day of epics, as above defined, is over; for though the action of spiritual forces on human affairs is still of supreme interest, their embodiment in concrete persons is no longer credible. Dryden had a scheme for using the guardian angels of nations, which came to nothing. Byron boldly proclaimed *Don Juan* the modern epic. Tennyson got no farther than " epic idylls." Mr. G. K. Chesterton has called Browning's *The Ring and the Book* the " great epic of the nineteenth century, for it is the great epic of the enormous importance of small things " ; but it could not by any means be squeezed into the definition given above. Mr. Thomas Hardy's *The Dynasts* is nearer to the old conception. Some critics do not distinguish so sharply between epic and **narrative** poem.

Dr. Garnett says that an epic is any narrative in verse not familiar or humorous, nor extremely brief. This would include such a poem as Morris's *Life and Death of Jason*, the very title of which proclaims that its "action" is not "one," and it is in fact Dr. Garnett's instance of the "artificial epic." Of the "national epic" he instances Homer, and the Finnish *Kalevala;* and of the intermediate class, partly national and partly artificial, the *Æneid* and *Lusiad*, Lucan's *Pharsalia*, Shelley's *Revolt of Islam*, and Tasso's *Jerusalem*. "Two great epic poets of the intermediate class have preserved and expressed the sentiment of their age, and its replies to the deepest questions which man can propound; they have clothed these abstractions with form, colour and music, and have lent fleeting opinion an adamantine immortality. These are Dante and Milton."

Epigram.—The Greek word meant an inscription, as for a monument, statue, or votive offering. Hence its marks are brevity and precision. The most famous of epigrams is that commemorating the Spartans who fell at Thermopylæ. Its very inadequate English version runs—

> Go, tell the Spartans, thou that passest by,
> That here, obedient to their laws, we lie.

The term was extended to include almost

EPIGRAM

any brief and pointed poem ; the Greek Anthology is their great store-house. A good English example is Lord Nugent's—

> I loved thee beautiful and kind,
>   And plighted an eternal vow ;
> So altered are thy face and mind,
>   'Twere perjury to love thee now.

Landor was a master of this form, and among modern poets Mr. William Watson. Martial sharpened the " point," and made it a " sting in the tail."

> Three things must epigrams, like bees, have all—
> A sting, and honey, and a body small.

Boileau provides a good instance, thus in English :

> Beneath this stone my wife doth lie ;
> She is at rest—and so am I.

Byron considered this of Samuel Rogers unsurpassable :

> Ward has no heart, they say ; but I deny it.
> He has a heart, and gets his speeches by it.

Here is an oriental epigram, as rendered by Leigh Hunt :

> Hamadan is my native place ;
>   And I must say, in praise of it,
> It merits, for its ugly face,
>   What everybody says of it.

> Its children equal its old men
> In vices and avidity,
> And they reflect the babes again
> In exquisite stupidity.

The word is now often used of any pointed remark.

Epithets.—The right use of epithets is a great secret of good style. Voltaire held the adjective the enemy of the noun. Shirley's foolish Caperwit thought otherwise—

> Adjectives! they're the flower, the grace of all our language.
> A well-chosen epithet doth give new soul
> To fainting poesy, and makes every verse
> A bride. With adjectives we bait our lines.

Quintilian is judicious as usual; their absence, he says, makes the style barren and uncomely; their excess produces something like an army with as many camp-followers as soldiers. Pope thus tells how the four elements were subdued to the use of men:

> He from the wond'ring furrow called the food,
> Taught to command the fire, control the flood,
> Draw forth the monsters of th' abyss profound,
> Or fetch th' aerial eagle to the ground.

Only important words are given epithets, and not all of them. Johnson took great pains to find apt epithets, but he had not

EPITHETS

Pope's tact in their use. Describing Wolsey's fall he writes:

> Now drops at once the pride of awful state,
> The golden canopy, the glittering plate,
> The regal palace, the luxurious board,
> The liveried army, and the menial horde.

The adjectives are all "just," but the effect is monotonous. Cp. George Eliot: "The slanting sunbeams shone through the transparent shavings that flew before the steady plane." Epithets are either "ornamental" or "essential." When Cowper describes a lady, "the mercer's plague, littering with unfolded silks the *polished* counter," and buying nothing, the polish adds nothing to the point, which is the lady's selfishness; the epithet is merely ornamental, adding a certain richness to the description. When Wordsworth, hearing the solitary reaper's song, exclaims—

> Oh hearken! for the vale *profound*
> Is overflowing with the sound—

the epithet is more than descriptive, for the deeper the vale, the more sonorous must be the song which overflows it. Wordsworth was rightly displeased when Scott misquoted his lines—

> The swan on *sweet* St. Mary's lake
> Floats double, swan and shadow—

for "still," which is essential to the picture. The epithet is conspicuously "essential" in such poetical phrases as Pindar's description of honey, "the harmless venom of the bee," where it transforms the meaning of its noun. Chapman has "solid flames" for jewels, "dry waves" for a crowd, "solid flood" for a mirror. Sir T. Browne describes glow-worms as "sublunary moons." "Soft ivory," for flesh, may be traced from Sidney, through Dekker and Cleveland, to Keats. Drummond has "bloods' liquid coral," and Whiting "the satyr's growing palaces." Keats has "the green and juicy hay," for grass. The stock epithet is equally at home in the Homeric epic and the English ballad. Achilles is always "swift-footed," whether his legs or his tongue are in question; and in our old ballads, as Macaulay says, "all the gold is red, and all the ladies are gay."

Essay.—"The essay is not to be cornered in a definition. For what genius could find a common denominator for essays so contrary in tendency as Locke on the Human Understanding and Lamb on Roast Pig?" Montaigne first used the name for his informal reflexions on himself and mankind. Locke's use is a piece of modesty, as disclaiming the dignity of an exhaustive treatise. Addison

ESSAY

contrasts those of his Spectators which are written with regularity and method with those others that run out into the wildness of those compositions which go by the name of essays. Bacon borrowed the name for a different thing. His *Essays* are indeed but short studies on subjects often great, but the extraordinary compression of thought and language, as of a synopsis covering the whole ground, gives them unique value for the stimulation of thought. Steele originated, and Addison developed the essay " as a device for reconciling fashion and virtue, industry and civil demeanour, philosophy and coffee-house tatlerdom, without the sanction of pulpit threats of damnation." The later stage of the essay, " the personal and lyrical phase," has Charles Lamb for its great luminary, with Hazlitt, Leigh Hunt, and later R. L. Stevenson as bright stars. Further varieties have been invented by Messrs. A. Birrell, E. V. Lucas, W. B. Yeats, and G. K. Chesterton. The historical essay, invented by Southey and adorned by Carlyle, was written by Macaulay with a brilliancy of colour and force of movement which have become proverbial. We are clearly a long way from the tame wildness of Addison. (The quotations above come from an article in the *Times Literary Supplement.*)

Ethic Dative.—The name is borrowed from classical grammar to describe the use of a pronoun as indicating the person remotely concerned: e.g. "he plucked *me* ope his doublet," where I am not at all closely connected with the action, and the pronoun is inserted merely to emphasize the speaker's veracity: I was there and I saw him do it. So in the sentence "Give *me* your present to one master Bassanio," "me" is clearly not the ordinary indirect object, but indicates that I am a person somehow interested in a transaction between you and Bassanio.

Euphemism is an inoffensive name for an unpleasant thing. Pope mentions a court preacher "who never mentions hell to ears polite;" he called it "a place which I think it not decent to name in so polite an assembly." Superstition may be a cause. The sailor felt on better terms with the Cape of Good Hope when it ceased to be called the Cape of Storms. The euphemisms for "death" are many: e.g. going west, passing away, joining the majority, kicking the bucket. A very unfeeling phrase for "burial" occurs in the *Spectator*. The widow tells of a visit from a friend on the very day her late lord had "gone into the country with Russel," where we have to remember that Russel is the fox in Chaucer, and that his country house is underground. The devil is disguised as his Satanic majesty, old Nick, the old boy. " Plain " is more polite than " ugly," and some elegant persons substitute for the vulgar " cheap " the stately " inexpensive." When euphemism is insincere, it is no part of good writing ; but it is often a deliberate form of **litotes,** as when a dangerous spot on the West Front was known as " unhealthy," and may be very effective.

Euphony is pleasing sound, and is therefore a mark of all good verse, unless it is discarded for special reasons. The accumulation of consonants, excessive alliteration, **sigmatism, hiatus,** a too irregular rhythm— these are some of its enemies : e.g. " But Bedlam still exists with its sage fetter " (Byron) : " piece meal | he gets | lands, and | spends as | much time " (Donne). Abrupt sounds are less euphonious than continuous sounds ; there is more music in long vowels than in short ones, in l, m, n, r, v, f, w than in p, t, k. Shelley delights in such words as " weave, woven, woof." But excessive care for euphony may lead to mere smoothness and lack of strength. Warton was surely wrong in his criticism of Spenser's line—" But was admired much of fools,|wómen,|and boys." He wanted to smoothen out the effective cross-rhythm by reading " women, fools, and boys." Byron has an ingenious stanza on the euphony of the Italian tongue:

I love the language, that soft bastard Latin,
  Which melts like kisses from a female mouth,
And sounds as if it should be writ on satin,
  With syllables which breathe of the sweet South,
And gentle liquids gliding all so pat in,
  That not a single accent seems uncouth,
Like our harsh northern whistling, grunting, guttural,
  Which we're obliged to hiss, and spit and sputter all.

The orator as well as the poet studies euphony; *voluptati aurium morigerari debet oratio* is a maxim of Cicero; and the precautions taken by the Greek orators are almost unbelievable in their nicety.

Euphuism is the style popularized by John Lyly in his romance of *Euphues*. Its chief marks are antithesis, alliteration, and elaborate illustrations drawn from the botany, zoology, and mineralogy of the Middle Ages: e.g. " It is the disposition of the thought that altereth the nature of the thing. The sun shineth upon the dunghill and is not corrupted; the diamond lieth in the fire and is not consumed; the crystal toucheth the toad and is not poisoned; the bird trochilus lieth by the mouth of the crocodile, and is not spoiled; a perfect wit is never bewitched with lewdness, neither enticed with lasciviousness." The word is less accurately used of any high-flown, periphrastic style.

EXPLETIVES

Expletives are words or phrases which add nothing to the sense ; of which profane oaths supply an obvious example. Rustics are apt to use phrases like " as a man may say "— which Butler laughs at in *Hudibras*—and even educated people are liable to excess in " do you see ? " But from a literary point of view the most interesting expletive is " to do " used as a mere auxiliary verb, with no intention of emphasis. This use was once quite common in all numbers and persons, and is still a lively provincialism. Spenser is full of it. So is the Authorized Version of the Bible : e.g. Rejoice with them that do rejoice : and they did all eat. Normal English now confines it to negative and interrogative sentences. Milton seems to be the first poet who avoided it. In the first four books of *Paradise Lost* I find only one instance of " did " in an affirmative sentence, and none of " do." Pope proscribed it as not **correct**. Johnson says that the words *do* and *did* " much degrade in present estimation the line that admits them." The reaction from eighteenth-century style to the earlier standards restored their use, but Lamb felt that while they have sometimes a good effect, their excess is objectionable. Shelley is full of them. Wordsworth admitted even into his highly wrought poem *Laodamia* the line " a generous cause a victim did demand."

F

Fable is a short **allegory**. It makes no pretence of dignity in style or originality in thought, but inculcates homely truths in a homely way. As Coleridge says, " there must be nothing but what is universally known and acknowledged." The characters are often animals; the convenience of this is that certain animals, e.g. the fox, have certain fixed characters, which need no previous explanation. They are very largely oriental in origin. Well-known examples are the Fox and the Grapes, the Man and the Bundle of Sticks, the Hare with many Friends. Addison says the fable is the least shocking way of giving advice : " We peruse the author for the sake of the story, and consider the precepts rather as our own conclusions, than his instructions." It may be doubted whether this is as true now as when it was written. We are more sophisticated than Addison's readers—his readers, I say, for of course Addison does not include himself in the " we." The word is also used in a different sense, for the plot or story of a drama or narrative poem. The critics of the eighteenth century were accustomed to judge of such things in separate compartments : e.g. fable, sentiments, diction, characters, etc.

Feminine Cæsura is a cæsura after an unaccented syllable : e.g. To err is human|, to forgive divine.

Feminine ending.—Iambic lines properly close on an accented syllable ; when an extra unstressed syllable is added, this is called a feminine ending : e.g. To be or not to be—that is the ques|tion. This is very common in dramatic blank verse ; it gives rapidity and a less formal rhythm. Shakespeare's later plays are full of it, and his successors write long passages without a stressed close to any line. Milton admits it freely in *Comus* and *Samson Agonistes* ; but it is quite rare in *Paradise Lost*, and the weight and dignity of the verse gains thereby. It is more frequent in the much freer verse of *Paradise Regained*, nearly half the examples being present participles. When this extra syllable occurs in rhymed verse, the result is **feminine rhyme**, also called double rhyme.

Figurative is equivalent to metaphorical, and opposed to literal. Many words which started with a literal sense have, by a metaphor, come to be used figuratively : e.g. to grasp, which can be an operation of the mind as well as of the hand. Some have lost the literal sense : e.g. to depend, which originally denoted the literal hanging of one thing on another, as in Spenser : " As on your boughs the icicles depend " ; even Shelley can write of " the depending leaf." An interesting example is " influence," which is properly a flowing on, and described the action of that subtle fluid which was supposed to flow from the stars and control human affairs. So the Lord asks Job " Canst thou bind the sweet influences of the Pleiades ? " This original sense was long alive in the poetical use of the word. When Milton wrote that ladies' eyes " rain influence," he was definitely likening them to stars.

Figures of Speech are methods of expressing a thought which make it more striking than the ordinary method, as when we say " Impossible ! " instead of " that is impossible " (ellipse), or " a thousand thanks " for " many thanks " (hyperbole). They are exceptional but not unnatural modes of expression. It was so natural for the young Goethe to express himself in similes and figures, that Dr. Gall assured him he was born to be a popular orator. The theory to which Quintilian and Addison have lent their authority, that figures were invented by the critics to palliate little errors in great writers, is really too absurd. They are naturally more common in the more emotional forms of composition, oratory and poetry. Their effective use depends largely on what we call good **taste**. Pope and Arbuthnot have an amusing discourse on their suitability to different sorts of persons. Aristotle had said that hyperbole was an ornament fit for young men of quality, and they add soldiers and seamen. " Periphrasis is the peculiar talent of country farmers ; the proverb and apologue of old men at their clubs ; the ellipse or speech by half-words, of ministers and politicians ; the aposiopesis of courtiers ; the litotes, or diminution, of ladies, whisperers and backbiters " ; etc. For the separate figures see : abstract for concrete, alliteration, anti-climax, antithesis, aposiopesis, apostrophe, bathos, chiasmus, climax, euphemism, hendiadys, hyperbole, hysteron proteron, innuendo, inversion, irony, litotes, meiosis, metaphor, metonymy, onomatopœia, oxymoron, paradox, paronomasia, periphrasis, personification, pleonasm, prolepsis, simile, syllepsis, synecdoche, tautology, zeugma.

Foot is the name given to the recurring group (or groups) of syllables that goes to compose a normal line of verse : e.g. John Gil|pin was|a cit|izen||of cre|dit and|renown. The word is impossible to define fully, on account of the subtle interlacing of **accent** and **quantity** in English verse. In this book we define feet by the number of syllables, and the position of the accent. See **Scansion,** and the separate articles on anapæst, dactyl, iamb, pyrrhic, spondee, tribrach, trochee. Coleridge wrote for his little son Derwent these lines illustrating the principal feet :

Tróchee|tríps from|lóng to|short ;
From long to long in solemn sort
Slów Spón|deé stálks ;| stróng foót || yet ill able
Éver to|cóme up with|Dáctyl tri|sýllable.
Iám|bics márch|from shórt|to lóng ;
With a leáp|and a bóund|the swift A|napæsts thróng.

Fourteener is the old English **iambic** line of fourteen syllables, making seven feet. Surrey was fond of writing it alternately with **Alexandrines,** but for some reason we find this arrangement disappoint the ear in an unpleasing manner. Chapman's fine translation of the *Iliad* is written in pairs of rhyming fourteeners : e.g.

As when about the silver moon, when air is free from wind,
And stars shine clear, to whose sweet beams high prospects and the brows
Of all steep hills and pinnacles thrust themselves up for shows,
And even the lowly valleys joy to glitter in their sight,
While the unmeasur'd firmament bursts to disclose her light,

FOURTEENER

And all the signs in heaven are seen that glad the shep-
 herd's heart ;
So many fires disclos'd their beams, made by the Trojan
 part,
Before the face of Ilion, and her bright turrets show'd.
A thousand courts of guard kept fires, and every guard
 allow'd
Fifty stout men, by whom their horse ate oats and hard
 white corn,
And all did wishfully expect the silver-thronèd morn.

G

General is opposed to particular or specific, as abstract to concrete. Generalization is a great pleasure of the philosophic mind, enabling it to deal with masses of otherwise unmanageable details. But the more general a notion is, the less vividly it is perceived by most minds; it soon leaves the senses behind; whereas poetry, as Milton said, is more simple and sensuous; it appeals to the mind directly through the senses. That is why Gray said that " circumstance [i.e. concrete detail] ever was and will be the life and essence of oratory and poetry." The critics of his day held details mean and generalities noble. " The business of the poet," says the sage in *Rasselas*, " is to examine not the individual, but the species; to remark general properties and large appearances. He does not number the streaks of the tulip "—and so on. But Gray was here, as often, ahead of his age. Sterne's originality is nowhere more striking than in his resolute avoidance of generalities and his insistence on detail. The broad generalities of Goldsmith's *Traveller* have been well contrasted with the detailed vigour of *Childe Harold*. Wordsworth taught that it was the poet's business to write with his eye on the object, and his successors have followed the advice; selection, not abstraction, is the method of poetry. Prose writers also must remember that the more concrete their statements, the more vigorous the effect. That a general truth may be expressed in concrete terms is shown by the familiar sentence: "According as men delight in battles, bull-fights, and combats of gladiators, so will they punish by hanging, burning, and crucifying." Modern critics would not urge us to substitute the generalized version: "In proportion as the manners, customs and amusements of a nation are cruel and barbarous, the regulations of their penal code will be severe." There is no doubt which statement is the more vivid. Ruskin somewhere apologized for having used the generic word "hound" to make his sentence prettier; whereas the creature in question was a flat-nosed bull-dog. And yet Ruskin himself is prudish enough to use "limbs" for "legs," like an American.

Genitive is the classical name for that case of a noun which we call possessive. As it does not always denote possession, the name genitive is convenient in English. "Cæsar's wife" is obviously the wife possessed by

Cæsar; but what is "Cæsar's praise"? It may mean (1) praise given to Cæsar, (2) praise given by Cæsar: e.g. (1) all were loud in Cæsar's praise, (2) Cæsar's praise was dear to his soldiers. In (1) it corresponds to a sentence "all praised Cæsar," Cæsar being *object*; in (2) to a sentence "Cæsar praised his soldiers," Cæsar being *subject*. Hence the distinction of *objective* and *subjective* genitives. There is a memorable play on this double use in one of FitzGerald's quatrains:

> O Thou, who Man of baser Earth did'st make,
> And ev'n with Paradise devise the Snake;
>   For all the Sin wherewith the Face of Man
> Is blacken'd—Man's forgiveness give—and take!

Goldsmith, in a very captious criticism of Hamlet's famous soliloquy—he calls it a heap of absurdities—maintains that "the oppressors' wrong" *ought* to mean wrong sustained by the oppressor, i.e. an objective genitive. We do not feel that now, the fact being that in modern English the subjective genitive is the livelier of the two.

Grub Street in London came to be known, about the end of the seventeenth century, as an abode of needy authors, too poor to live in better quarters, and prepared usually to write anything for anybody at almost any pay. It supplied material for constant and very unsympathetic comment to Pope and Swift, who never themselves experienced privation. Johnson, who in his years of penury was very familiar with its denizens, succeeded in emerging and making the name of professional author for the first time respectable. The name was changed to Milton Street in 1830. The nearest modern equivalent is the much more pretentious " Bohemia," which is not a locality but rather a social status; and one does not think of the Bohemian as a hard worker, which the Grub Street hack often was.

H

Hemistich is a half-verse, occurring irregularly among whole verses. It is obviously convenient in dramatic poetry, and does not offend the ear. But in poetry proper, whether blank or heroic couplets, it has a very disappointing effect. Cowley introduced it sparingly into his epic *Davideis*, in imitation of the incomplete lines which are fairly frequent in Virgil's *Æneid*; he did not believe that these lines would have been filled out if Virgil had lived to revise his poem. Lesser poets have found the introduction of hemistichs a particularly easy and recognizable way of being Virgilian. The word is also used in the more obvious sense of one half of a whole verse divided by the cæsura.

Hendiadys is the use of two nouns joined by " and " where one is adjectival in force. The figure is common in Virgil, and Tennyson has attempted it: " the marble threshold strown with gold and scattered coinage," i.e. scattered gold coins; " served with female hands and hospitallity," i.e. hospital female hands; "waving to him white hands and courtesy," i.e. courteous white hands. It is noticeable that in each case there is an epithet as well as the two nouns. Puttenham illustrates the figure in its barest form :

> The Nubians marching with their armèd carts,
> And fleeing afar with venom and with darts—

i.e. venomous darts; and Shakespeare has such phrases as " tediousness and process " (for " tedious process "), " flint and hardness," even " slow and moving " for " slowly moving." Milton writes of Satan : " With joy and tidings fraught, to hell he now returned " —for " joyful tidings." Horace Walpole supplies an exceptional example. In discussing the wording of some lines he suggests " steal and adopt " as an alternative for " by stealth adopt."

Heroic = epical. " An heroic poem," says Dryden, " is certainly the greatest work of human nature. The beauties and perfections of the other [tragedy] are but mechanical; those of the **epic** are more noble." He thus defines **heroic verse** : " The English verse which we call heroic consists of no more than ten syllables " ; i.e. the standard five-foot iambic line. When this is unrhymed, we have **blank verse,** true heroic in *Paradise Lost.* When rhymed in pairs it makes the **heroic couplet,** first found in Chaucer's *Legend of Good Women,* and the metre of most of the *Canterbury Tales.* This couplet ousted

octosyllabics as the staple of English verse, rivalled the stanza forms for two centuries, was the tyrant of English prosody for two centuries more, and is still one of the very greatest metres for every purpose but pure lyric (Saintsbury). Chaucer wrote it with admirable lightness and freedom; so in modern times did his disciple William Morris; Dryden gave it power and impetus; but the brilliant form perfected by Pope regularly closes the sense with every couplet, and avoids long pauses elsewhere; hence its monotony in a long poem. See **Enjambment.** For the history of the heroic couplet see Sir Sidney Colvin's *Keats*, pp. 94 foll.

Hexameters are lines of six feet, but it is convenient to reserve the word for dactylic hexameters, consisting of **dactyls** and **spondees,** written by old Greeks and Romans, and by modern English and Germans. There are materials for a long essay on the attempts made to write pleasing hexameters in English, from Spenser's friend Gabriel Harvey, down to the Poet Laureate. The present position seems to be, that instead of getting hexameters to please our ears, we must get ears capable of being pleased with hexameters. Ears differ dreadfully in the matter. Sara Coleridge liked the German sort, but hated the English (whereas her uncle Southey held he had proved them " in no respect dissuited to the genius of our language "); but Tennyson hated the German even more. The mere predominance of consonants in our tongue forbids us ever to compete with Homer. Here is the first line of Longfellow's *Evangeline*:

Thís is the|fórest pri|maéval, the|múrmuring|pínes and the|hémlócks—

where the clash of accent and quantity in the second foot is not lovely. Charles Kingsley's *Andromeda* is much less painful: e.g.

Ónward they|cáme in their|jóy and a|roúnd them the| lámps of the|séa-nýmphs.

The spondees are a difficulty, shirked in the two lines quoted, but bravely faced by Poe in the following:

Why ask !|Whoever|yet saw|moneymade|out of a|fat old Jew, or|downright|upright|nutmegs|out of a|pine-knot?

Hexameters turn up oddly at times: e.g. " Please will you get me my muff ? I've left it behind in the carriage "; or " Smoking is not allowed in the walks and grounds of the college." Dr. Johnson once slyly slipt in a hexameter which most readers ignore: " as Homer says, ' nothing but rumour has reached, and who has no personal knowledge." The English Bible supplies several: e.g.

"Husbands love your wives, and be not bitter against them," the spondees of which contrast with the dactylic run of "How art thou fallen from heaven, O Lucifer, son of the morning!" Longfellow's lines scan purely by accent. Here are two which take account of quantity as well:

Sudbury town stands here. In an old-world region around it
Tall, dark pines, like spires, with above them a murmur of umbrage
Guard for us all deep peace (Mallock).

Virgil succeeded in moulding the stiff Latin tongue to a magnificent metre on the model of the Homeric hexameter. It would be hazardous to deny that some genius might obtain a similar result with English.

Hiatus means a gap, and is used especially of what Dryden calls "a most horrible ill-sounding gap" due to open vowels (see **elision**); he avoided hiatus in his translation of the *Æneid*, but in this, as in other matters, his practice did not always square with his theory of what is best. He censures Chapman's line—"The army's plague, the strife of kings," because of the hiatus after "the." Pope felt that elision might in certain cases sound worse than hiatus, and says the ear ought to decide. He gives as an example of excessive hiatus—" Though oft the ear the open vowels tire." It is not well to cure hiatus in speech by inserting an r sound : e.g. " I had no idear of it." Some of the most scrupulous Greek writers avoided hiatus even in their prose, but the Roman critics agree that it may give an air of not unpleasing negligence, indicating a greater care for things than words. The sensitiveness thus indicated, so remote from our carelessness in such matters, is probably connected with the practice of hearing new works recited in public, instead of reading them at home.

Humour.—The great English humorists are Chaucer, Shakespeare, Sterne, and Carlyle. Humour was conspicuously lacking in Spenser, Milton, Wordsworth, and Shelley. No humorist is greater than Cervantes. Tennyson held that humour was generally most fruitful in the highest and most solemn human spirits. Mr. John Bailey doubts if it is compatible with achievement of the very highest order, and marshals a formidable list of great non-humorists—St. Paul, Mahomet, Alexander the Great, Napoleon, Dante [Tennyson says he is full of humour], Milton, Phidias, Michael Angelo. It will be noticed that Milton is the one undisputed writer among them. Addison, himself master of a very delicate humour, despairing of a definition, gives instead an ingenious genealogy. Truth, he says, was founder of the family, and father of Good Sense. His son was Wit, who married Mirth, and Humour was their child. This is worth thinking over, but Carlyle's account of it is much richer. " The essence of humour is sensibility ; warm, tender fellow-feeling with all forms of existence. Nay, we may say that unless seasoned and purified by humour, sensibility is apt to run wild." He goes on to quote Schiller : " The last perfection of our faculties is that their activity, without ceasing to be sure and earnest, becomes *sport*. True humour is sensibility, in the most catholic and deepest sense ; but it is this *sport* of sensibility ; wholesome and perfect therefore ; as it were, the playful teazing fondness of a mother to her child." Again, it is " thinking in jest while feeling in earnest " (G. Eliot), or " the faculty which always keeps us in mind of the absurdity which is the shadow of sublimity " (L. Stephen). The humorist can contemplate without contempt the weakness of himself and others. He is the true optimist. See also on **Wit.**

Hyperbole is exaggeration in expression : e.g. rivers of blood and hills of slain. A Greek critic says that in using hyperbole we lie without deceiving, and without trying to deceive. Another says that we use it in our

HYPERBOLE

arguments to strike those who will not listen to what is possible. A famous instance of this is the Gospel saying about the camel and the needle's eye. Cp. Tertullian's *certum est quia impossibile*. It is thus akin to **paradox**. In poetry it is part of the language of emotion: e.g.

> So frowned the mighty combatants that Hell
> Grew darker at their frown.

Wordsworth notices how the passion of the writer justifies these lines of Montrose on Charles I:

> But since thy loud-tongued blood demands supplies
> More from Briareus' hands than Argus' eyes,
> I'll sing thy obsequies with trumpets' sounds,
> And write thy epitaph with blood and wounds.

But we must be convinced of the sincerity of the passion. Cleveland's lines on the youth lamented by Milton in *Lycidas* are mere fustian—

> Our tears shall seem the Irish seas,
> We, floating islands, living Hebrides.

Hyperbole is often used with comic effect. Gladstone was once delighted to hear a street boy remark to a very tall pedestrian: " I say, guv'nor, if you was to lie down, you'd be 'arf ways 'ome."

HYSTERON PROTERON

Hysteron proteron is a reversal of the actual time-order of events, for the sake of emphasis. Let us " die," says Virgil, " and rush into the fray," thus emphasizing the speaker's resolution to fight to the uttermost. So Palamon's love for Emily is so hot that he is willing to take even death for his sentence—" Therefore I axe deeth and my juwyse." Cp. " Who is worthy to open the book and to loose the seals thereof ? " (*Revelation* v. 2).

> The Antoniad, the Egyptian admiral [flag-ship],
> With all their sixty, fly and turn the rudder.

Pope, feeling that no self-respecting epic could do without a hysteron proteron, has neatly supplied one in his mock epic, *The Rape of the Lock*. At waking-time, he says—

> Thrice rung the bell, the slipper knocked the ground,
> And the pressed watch returned a silver sound.

The waker would of course make sure of the time before ringing or knocking on the floor for the servant.

I

Iamb is a two-syllable **foot**, with the accent on the second syllable : e.g. To bé|or nót|to bé. Iambic lines are the commonest of all in English verse ; but, for the sake of variety, trochees, spondees, and pyrrhics are often substituted ; and many writers allow also three-syllable feet. See **Scansion**.

Idyll.—" When civilization becomes complicated, and concentrates itself in cities, there arises by reaction a peculiar pleasure in contemplating the simple, half animal life that has been left behind, and this pleasure has left a great mark on literature " (Abbott and Seeley). The idyll is a **pastoral** ; also it is usually short, and the interest of the events described is picturesque rather than dramatic. Theocritus first wrote such poems, dealing with the rustic life of Sicily, to please the highly civilized Alexandrians. Virgil's *Eclogues* or *Bucolics* were written in imitation, but also with a genuine love of the subject, whereas the many modern pastorals, such as Pope's, are more often a further imitation of Virgil than real studies of country life. Tennyson's *English Idylls* are an attempt to

IDYLL—IMPERSONAL CONSTRUCTION

restore sincerity of treatment. His *Idylls of the King* abandon the rustic setting altogether, but retain much of the picturesqueness proper to the idyll. They are episodes of an unwritten epic. The word is sometimes stretched to include tales of country life like George Eliot's *Silas Marner*. See also **Poetry, forms of**.

Impersonal Construction is used to express an action without naming the actor: e.g. "now was fought eagerly on both sides." Milton has here imitated in prose a common Latin construction which he has also admitted to *Paradise Lost*—" Forthwith on all sides to his aid was run." The Poet Laureate has " No longer to high Paphos now 'twas sailed." The old Romance of Merlin supplies an instance of the more English idiom:

> There was fleeing and withstanding,
> Tiring, tugging, and overthrowing.

Cp. "and there was hurrying to and fro" (Byron), and "then came sudden alarms; hurryings to and fro, etc." (De Quincey).

Innuendo is the method of suggesting instead of openly stating what is meant. Bain quotes the remark made on a member of Parliament: "He did his party all the harm in his power: he spoke for it and voted against it." This indirect way of saying that he was a bad speaker is highly effective. So is Pope's line on the City Poet's verses descriptive of the Lord Mayor's Show :

> Now night descending, the gay scene is o'er ;
> But lives in Settle's numbers one day more.

The bard's immortality is limited to a day. The *Spectator's* acknowledgments to contributors contain this item : " The letter of P. S., who desires either to have it printed entire, or committed to the flames," with the comment " not to be printed entire." The usage shows in a small way the immense value of suggestion ; the mind is led to contribute something beyond what is written, and delights in sharing, as it were, in the act of composition.

Inversion is the placing of words out of the usual grammatical order, and has three chief forms (1) putting the adjective after the noun, (2) putting the object before the verb, (3) putting the preposition after its noun. Gray's poems abound with examples of the second form. When it is used merely for the sake of rhyme or metre, it usually indicates laziness or lack of skill. Wordsworth blames Scott for his many liberties of this sort : as a device for heightening the style it is simply bad writing. " We were whipt at Westminster," says Dryden, " if we used it twice together" for the sake of the rhyme. The notion that it gives dignity, as Cowper held, seems to come from its suggestion of Latin style, in which the object commonly precedes the verb. But the Poet Laureate holds that it is of the essence of good style. "In ordinary speech the words follow a common order prescribed by use, and if that does not suit the sense, correction is made by vocal intonation : but the first thing a writer must do is to get his words in the order of his ideas, as he wishes them to enter the reader's mind ; and when such an arrangement happens not to be the order of common speech, it may be called a grammatical inversion. . . . The best simple writers have the art of making the common grammatical forms obey their ideas." That is the true gospel. Here is the famous beginning of Pope's *Iliad* :

> Achilles' wrath, to Greece the direful spring
> Of woes unnumber'd, heavenly goddess, sing !

Calverley's hexameter has the less effective order : " Sing, O daughter of heaven, of Peleus' son, of Achilles." Homer's own first word is " wrath," and that is the subject of the poem. Cp. the opening of *Paradise Lost*.

Irony is a method of statement in which the contrary of what is said is to be under-

IRONY

stood. It is quite common in ordinary speech: e.g. "A fine government we've got!" Famous examples are: Job's remark to his friends, "No doubt but ye are the people, and wisdom shall die with you"; Elijah's mocking praise of Baal; Antony's speech in *Julius Cæsar*. Sustained irony may be very effective; "it is a form of restraint," says Professor Dowden, "like the censure of the press forcing one to say things in the most dexterous way"; but when it is overdone, as sometimes in Swinburne's prose, it is merely annoying. Goethe trenchantly observes that "in the long run it annoys the clear-sighted, perplexes the foolish, yet appeals to the majority who imagine themselves cleverer than others." But he admired the irony of *The Vicar of Wakefield*. Swift is the greatest English master of sustained irony. His *Modest Proposal* for relieving an Irish famine by using the starving children for food is argued with the calm deliberation of a philanthropic statesman. He certainly used irony as "a form of restraint," so as to write calmly of things which made his blood boil. Fielding used it just as an effective form of statement. His *Jonathan Wild the Great* describes the career of an utter scoundrel in terms appropriate to (say) Napoleon. Much of what is called Thackeray's cynicism is really ironical statement of the truly pathetic. Jane Austen is a unique example of a female ironist. **Dramatic irony** is the device of putting words into a speaker's mouth which have for the audience a meaning not intended by the speaker. Sophocles used it with tremendous effect in *Œdipus Tyrannus*, and Shakespeare's Pandarus proposes that, if ever Troilus and Cressida prove false to one another, all goers-between should be called Pandars, and all false women Cressids.

K

Kailyard School. See under **Dialect.**

L

Lake School or " Lakers " is the misleading name given to certain poets who, at the beginning of the nineteenth century, lived among the lakes of Cumberland; Wordsworth, Coleridge, and Southey were the chief of them. Wordsworth and Coleridge had a good deal of theory in common, though their poems are very different in character, but Southey was no member of the alleged school; he highly disapproved both of Wordsworth's theory and of his practice. " The term arose," says Coleridge, " from our not hating or envying one another." It was seized on with avidity by Byron, who considered their poetry vulgar twaddle. " I hate and abhor," he wrote to Murray, " that puddle of water-worms whom you have taken into your troop . . . pond-poets." And again : " the Lakers, who whine about nature because they live in Cumberland." Hazlitt, in a few vicious pages of his *Lectures on the English Poets*, formulates their alleged principles : " They were for bringing poetry back to its primitive simplicity and state of nature, as Rousseau was for bringing society back to the state of nature: so that the only thing remarkable left in the world by this change would be the persons who had produced it": and so on. Such errors can be made even by capable critics, when they take ill-tempered and one-sided views. Jeffrey in the *Edinburgh Review* had been a ferocious assailant of the " school," but eventually came to value Wordsworth highly; and they had enlightened support from De Quincey, John Wilson (Christopher North), Lamb, and Leigh Hunt. Even Hazlitt was not always so mordant as in the passage quoted.

Leonine Verses are Latin hexameters or pentameters, with internal rhyme at the cæsura : e.g.

> Permutant *mores* homines, cum dantur *honores*:
> Corde stat *inflato* pauper honore *dato*.

Trench, in the introduction to his *Sacred Latin Poetry*, gives copious specimens of their varieties. They were immensely popular in the Middle Ages. Here is another, for which—the sentiment, not the infamous metre—Puttenham says the author ought to have his eyes picked out with pins, " or worse handled if worse could be devised " :

> Fallere, flere, nere, mentiri, nilque tacere,
> Hæc quinque vere statuit Deus in muliere.

LEONINE VERSES—LIMERICK

Thus in English—

> To cheat, weep, spin, and lie,
> To hold her tongue for no man—
> These five gifts, verily,
> Has God bestowed on woman.

Parnell turned Belinda's toilet, from *The Rape of the Lock*, into leonine hexameters. To use the phrase for Latin verse with only final rhyme is very confusing, and not admitted by the *N.E.D.*; but Gray and Warton, both men of sense and learning, did so.

Limerick is a name for the stanza in which Lear wrote his *Book of Nonsense* (1846).

> There was a young lady of Tyre,
> Who swept the loud chords of a lyre;
> At the sound of each sweep
> She enraptured the deep,
> And enchanted the city of Tyre.

Later adepts have changed the character of the Limerick by introducing a new rhyme-word in the last line. The resulting gain in epigrammatic point is made at the expense of the more solemn fatuity of the original form, as in this:

> There was a young lady of Rio,
> Who once played in Haydn's Grand Trio;
> But her skill being scanty
> She played it *andante*
> Though it should be *allegro con brio*.

The form first appeared in *History of Sixteen Wonderfvl Old Women* (1821).

Litotes, or **meiosis,** is deliberate understatement for the sake of effect. It is akin to **irony** and opposed to **hyperbole.** When St. Paul called himself " a citizen of no mean city," he referred to the provincial metropolis of Tarsus. The figure is common in ordinary discourse : e.g. not half bad=very good. See also **Euphemism.** Among savages it is sometimes a form of politeness ; Livingstone tells of certain Africans who, in offering an ox as a present, would say " here is a little piece of bread for you." Its literary use is often satirical in intention : e.g. Pope's lines—

> Narcissa's nature, tolerably mild,
> To make a wash would hardly stew a child.

Some writers confine litotes to such forms as " not unaccompanied " for " accompanied " ; these are very common in Wordsworth.

Lyric is primarily a poem meant to be sung. (It is interesting to find this sense alive still in the play-bills of " musical comedy.") The **ballad** is a popular form of lyric. The highly finished lyric is of moderate length, concise but perspicuous and musical in expression, and often extremely personal in tone. It is a revelation of joys or sorrows keenly felt

LYRIC

by the poet: e.g. Burns's love songs, and Shelley's shorter poems. Gray says—and there could be no better authority—that the lyric style, with its flights of fancy, ornaments, and harmony of sound, is in its nature superior to every other style, and for that very reason it could not be borne in a work of great length. Our emotions, like our muscles, require periods of repose. The lyric has a tendency to mix itself with other forms of poetry. *The Ancient Mariner* is in subject a narrative poem, but it has the lilt of song, not the steady tone of the reciter. Browning invented a form of poems called *Dramatic Lyrics*. " Victor Hugo carried all his lyric passion into an epic presentation, in detached scenes, of the life of humanity—*La Légende des Siècles* " (Dowden). Milton is a remarkable example of a master of lyric style who threw it completely from him when he came to write epic. The **ode, elegy,** and **sonnet** are special forms of the lyric.

M

Macaronic Verse has two senses : (1) verse in which two or more languages are intermixed; (2) said to be more " accurate," verse made up largely of native words turned into Latin or Greek forms. It was first written by Italians of the fifteenth and sixteenth centuries, and still appeals to humorous scholars from the incongruity of its forms, or the opportunity of setting classical tags in comic connections : " it is like freeing a solemn schoolmaster to join in the antics of his boys " (Leigh Hunt). Drummond of Hawthornden is the reputed author of a macaronic poem *Polemo-Middinia*, describing a rustic fight, and containing such phrases as *lassas kissare bonæas*, to kiss the bonny lasses ; *girnans more divelli*, grinning like the devil. The best known modern example is the *Comic Latin Grammar:*

Patres conscripti took a boat and went to Philippi.
Trumpeter unus erat qui coatum scarlet habebat.
Stormum surgebat, et boatum oversetebat,
Omnes drownerunt, quia swim-away non potuerunt
Excipe John Periwig tied up to the tail of a dead pig.

The metre is **hexameter,** with the mediæval

internal rhyme known as **leonine.** A quite recent writer has produced a *jeu d'esprit* called the *Bankolidaïd*, beginning " Jam Whit-Monday adest ; ex Newington Causeway the costers. . . ." Macaronics must not be confused with the " pedantesque " style found (e.g.) in Rabelais, which turns classical words into native forms : " If by fortune there be rarity or penury of pecune in our marsupies, and that they be exhausted of ferruginean metal for the shot, we dimit our codices, and oppignerate our vestiments, whilst we præstolate the coming of the tabellaries from the penates and patriotic lares " (Urquhart): i.e. if our purses lack money, we get rid of our books, pledge our clothes, and anticipate our patrimony. O. W. Holmes has an ingenious poem beginning :

> In candent ire the solar splendour flames ;
> The foles, languescent, pend from arid rames ;
> His humid front the cive, anheling, wipes,
> And dreams of erring on ventiferous ripes.

Machinery, says Pope, " is a term invented by the critics, to signify that part which the deities, angels or demons are made to act in a poem." Derived from the mechanical contrivance used by the Greeks to introduce a deity on the stage, it belongs properly to tragedy ; but Homer's constant introduction of deities in the action of the *Iliad* has led to its being used chiefly of the **epic.** The supernatural persons were called " machines"; Dryden says that " Milton's heavenly machines are many, and his human persons are but two." Pope's sylphs in *The Rape of the Lock* are a happy travesty of the epic machinery. Dr. Watts tells us that the blessed Spirit allowed Bible writers the privilege of " the introduction of machines on great occasions ; the Divine licence in this is admirable and surprising. Eliphaz—in the book of *Job*—introduces a machine in a vision : ' Fear came upon me, trembling on all my bones, the hair of my flesh stood up ; a Spirit passed by and stood still, but its form was indiscernible ; an image before mine eyes ; and silence ; then I heard a voice saying, Shall mortal man be more just than God ? ' " This is far removed from the notion of mechanism. Cp. Mr. Thomas Hardy's *The Dynasts*.

Madrigal, in its literary sense, is a short lyric usually dealing with love : e.g. Shakespeare's " Take oh take those lips away," or " Tell me where is fancy bred."

Meiosis. See **Litotes.**

Masques were introduced from Italy as a form of court entertainment under Henry VIII. They allowed king and courtiers to satisfy the universal delight in " dressing up."

MASQUES

The earliest masques consisted only of music, dancing, and dumb-show, and did not present any consecutive story. But under James I, when the masque was in its full glory, poets like Ben Jonson, Daniel, and William Browne provided the songs and dialogue, the music might be written by Henry Lawes, and the very elaborate stage devices contrived by a great architect like Inigo Jones. Bacon made a *Masque of the Marriage of the Thames and the Rhine* for the marriage of the enchanting Princess Elizabeth to the Elector Palatine ; and his short essay on the subject shows his practical interest in such things, though he begins and ends by calling them " toys." They always appealed most to the eye and the musical ear. Milton's famous *Comus* is not really characteristic ; though it has spectacular and musical attractions, its chief charm lies in the lovely poetry. Hartley Coleridge remarks that masques bore the same relation to *The Faerie Queene* as the Greek tragedies to the poems of Homer ; they were highly picturesque and even beautiful works, but lacked the artistic unity of classical models. There was often an Anti-Masque as well, a more or less humorous parody of the serious entertainment. Ben Jonson's *Masque of Christmas* has such personages as Minced Pie and Baby Cake.

Metaphor is an implied comparison, whereas **simile** is a comparison stated as such: e.g. the ship ploughs the waves. The corresponding simile would be: the ship cuts the waves as a plough cleaves the soil. "Metaphor is a great excellence in style," says Johnson, "when used with propriety, for it gives you two ideas for one;—conveys the meaning more luminously, and generally with a perception of delight." Thus Attila is described as the scourge of God, Chaucer as the morning-star of song. Metaphors are of two kinds—radical and poetical. Radical metaphors are a necessary part of all language. Locke first clearly stated that " in all languages the names which stand for things that fall not under our senses, had their first rise from sensible ideas"; the names of abstract notions are developed by metaphor from those of concrete notions. Thus "spirit" originally meant "breath," and to comprehend meant to grasp literally. Such words tend in time to lose all suggestion of the literal sense; the metaphor dies; but in this process the language loses much of its vividness. So the artist in language delights to quicken the metaphor and present a picture instead of a smudge. It is this sort of feeling which makes some people—to take a rather trivial example—careful to say "*in* these circumstances" (not *under*), because circumstances are literally what surrounds us, and we cannot be *under* them. On the other hand, the common vice of mixed metaphor arises from insensitiveness to the literal meaning of words and phrases. Castlereagh's effort is famous : " And now, sir, I must embark into the feature on which this question chiefly hinges." Even De Quincey could write : " Years that were far asunder were bound together by subtle links derived from a common root." Grant that the metaphor in " derive " is dead : there remains the incongruity of a root producing links. Such writing in many modern writers is both sloppy and pretentious. Poetical metaphors are a principal weapon of the poet and the orator ; they are " the life of poetry or prose " ; they may be of great value for the explanation of an idea : e.g. All great empires contain the seeds of their own dissolution. They may grip the imagination with an astonishing force. Æschylus's description of the beacon-fire as " a great beard of flame " remains with many who remember perhaps little else of the *Agamemnon*. On the abuse of metaphor see **Conceits.**

Metaphysical poets is a description fastened by Johnson on the highly intellectual poets of the early seventeenth century, especially Donne, Cowley, and Cleveland.

METAPHYSICAL—METONYMY

Dryden had said of Donne: "He affects the metaphysics, not only in his satires, but in his amorous verse, where Nature only should reign." Here is an example of the sort of thing. Cowley compares a lover, burnt up by his affection, to Egypt, which is watered not from heaven but by the Nile—

> The fate of Egypt I sustain,
> And never feel the dew of rain
> From clouds which in the head appear;
> But all my too much moisture owe
> To overflowings of the heart below.

The **conceit** is characteristic, but the statement is quite false; no reader of Cowley's "love poems" will admit that his heart had anything to say to their manufacture. But his learning and his acuteness may give us a certain intellectual pleasure, which is perhaps what Johnson meant by "metaphysical." In Donne's poems, on the other hand, the very outrageousness of the conceits is constantly expressive of a fiery emotion. Johnson notices that Milton tried the metaphysical style only in his lines upon Hobson the carrier, and thereafter disdained it. There is much of it in Dryden's early poems.

Metonymy means a change of name. We often call things not by their own names but by the name of something connected with them: e.g. the crown = royalty, the mitre =

METONYMY—MOCK-HEROIC

office of bishop, red tape = routine of office. In these cases the substituted word is a symbol. Or the instrument may be put for the agent : e.g. the pen is mightier than the sword, i.e. writers have more influence than soldiers. A common form of metonymy is putting the container for the thing contained : e.g. the bottle = alcoholic drink, the purse = money. There is nothing " wrong " in saying " the kettle boils " ; cp. he keeps a good table, he drank the cup, they smote the city. " From the cradle to the grave," " the palace and the cottage," are similar. Again, the author is often put for his works : e.g. they have Moses and the prophets ; " Bradshaw " is a railway guide ; and when treasury notes were first issued during the Great War, they were known as " Bradburys," from the signature engraved on them. This figure is a favourite with sporting scribes, who like to call a football " the oval " or " the leather."

Mock-heroic style is the converse of burlesque, and consists in the use of dignified and high-sounding language in the description of trivial things and actions. Pope's *The Rape of the Lock* is a perfect example. So is Gray's poem about the cat and the gold fishes. Dryden's *MacFlecknoe* is the first English poem of the kind. Garth's *Dispensary* owes much to the amusing *Lutrin* of Boileau. The earliest is the pseudo-Homeric *Batrachomyiomachia*, or Battle of the Frogs and Mice, described after the manner of the *Iliad*.

Monosyllables are characteristic of the English language. Professor H. Bradley notices that very few others can write whole pages almost exclusively in them, and contrasts the phrase " of two good men " with its Latin equivalent *duorum bonorum virorum*. Brevity and vigour may result; it is a true observation that the proverb " first come first served " is far more effective than the French *premier venu premier moulu*, whereas *bon jour bonne euvre* beats " the better the day, the better the deed." Cp. live and learn. But their staccato effect and frequent lack of sonority is a trial to writers whose ears are full of the polysyllabic magnificence of Greek and Latin. Camden says they are fit only for expressing the first conceits of the mind, or *Intentionalia*. Shaftesbury never wrote more than nine consecutive, and refused to end a sentence with a crowd of them. Chapman might sing their praise in the lines prefixed to his *Iliad*; but Dryden calls them " the dead weight of our mother tongue "; and Pope condemns writers who let " ten low words oft creep in one dull line "—where, in condemning he has illustrated the usage, and surely justified it for the purpose of a biting rebuke. In skilled hands monosyllables are capable of all effects, except perhaps such rapid magnificence as we find in Shakespeare's " the multitudinous seas incarnadine." In Ben Jonson's noble line on Shakespeare—" He was not of an age, but for all time "—there are only three words that are not " low "; and Drayton's miraculous sonnet —" Since there's no help, come let us kiss and part "—contains but seventeen words of more than one syllable, and only one of them has more than two. By cunning selection they may be highly expressive, as in Dyer's—

> With easy course
> The vessels glide ; unless their speed be stopped
> By dead calms that oft lie on those smooth seas,
> While every zephyr sleeps.

Shelley and Swinburne revel in their melodious use. A line like Morris's " and the first of the days was as near to the end that I sought as the last " illustrates the fact that many of our " low " monosyllables are in pronunciation so closely attached to the following word as to give a polysyllabic effect. In the beautiful use of words, a difficulty overcome is a new beauty; as usual, it is the less accomplished workman who finds fault with his tools. See more in the Appendix of *A Companion to Diaconus.*

Muse.—The Muses are to us the personified powers which inspire the different kinds of poetry. The Greeks who invented them conceived them as minor goddesses, and gave them charge also of History, Dancing, and Astronomy, thus completing " the Nine." The following lines are based on an epigram of Wither's :

> The acts of ages past doth Clio write,
> The tragedy's Melpomene's delight,
> Thalía is with comedies contented,
> Euterpe first the lyric song invented,
> Terpsichore doth lead the choric dance,
> Sweet Eràto sings lovers' dalliance,
> Calliope on epic verses dwells,
> The secrets of the stars Urania tells,
> Polyhymnia decks with words sublime the hymn,
> And great Apollo shares with all of them.

Homer begins the *Iliad* by calling on the Muse for inspiration, asking her, in fact, to compose the poem ; and later writers have thought it good manners or modesty to do likewise. A writer on the sugar-cane has this wonderful invocation : " Now Muse, let's sing of rats." Milton, at the beginning of his Christian epic, seriously invokes the Heavenly Muse as a personage more august than the pagan goddesses, in fact the power which inspired the Hebrew prophets. Even Wordsworth, for all his anti-classical bias, could hail the Muses as the sole survivors

MUSE

of Olympus. Byron has a characteristic touch at the beginning of *Don Juan*, iii: " Hail, Muse! *et cetera*—We left Juan sleeping." By an obvious **metonymy,** " Muse " is used to mean a kind of poetry : e.g. " he chose a mournful muse, soft pity to infuse." It is more strange as synonymous with a poet, as in *Lycidas* 19 ; this use occurs also in Spenser, Shakespeare, Dryden, and Gray.

N

Narrative Poetry would include all poems—except dramas—which tell a story; but the epic and the ballad are types so distinct that they are usually excluded. Narrative poems have as a rule neither the length nor the artistic unity of the epic; they are longer and often more stately than the ballad: but again some of the best are humorous: e.g. many of Chaucer's *Canterbury Tales*. It is permissible to disagree with George Wyndham's saying that Shakespeare's *Rape of Lucrece* is the only romantic story in English rhyme, worthy the name of literature, between Chaucer and Keats. Professor Saintsbury's *Caroline Poets* provides some which are at least interesting, and there are readers who find Chamberlayne's *Pharonnida*, with all its faults, even more than that: Dryden's *Fables* are presumably not " literature," and *The Rape of the Lock* is certainly not romantic, but is not *The Ancient Mariner* both ? Keats is a great master in *The Eve of St. Agnes, Isabella*, and *Lamia*. Mrs. Browning has written a long novel in verse—*Aurora Leigh*. William Morris, Tennyson, and Matthew

NARRATIVE POETRY—NOMINATIVE ABSOLUTE

Arnold are accomplished writers of the narrative poem, and there is no better example of constructive power in closely knit narrative than Sir Samuel Ferguson's *Conary*.

Nominative Absolute.—When a noun or pronoun, instead of being subject or object to a finite verb, is subject to a participle, the words forming a phrase which hangs loose to the rest of the sentence, the phrase is called a nominative absolute : e.g. these things being so, why should we deceive ourselves ? she failing in her promise, I will withdraw mine : this done, he retired. Sometimes the participle is omitted : e.g. Fair play [given], he cared na deils a boddle (Burns). In old English the absolute case was the dative; in Latin it is the ablative, but it is strange to read in a history of English literature that Tusser is full of ablative absolutes. Milton, probably influenced by the Latin, has "him destroyed . . . all this will soon follow"; but the nominative is quite common in Shakespeare, and is now regularly used. "Absolute" is opposed to "relative"; the absolute noun has not the usual definite relation to the rest of the sentence. If an absolute participle has no noun for its subject, it illustrates the ugly error known as "unrelated participle": e.g. touching a secret lock, the door opened. George Meredith writes "Meeting General Pierson, the latter rallied him," where the relation of "meeting" to "him" is unusual, and the form of the sentence is objectionable. The second couplet of Tennyson's *Locksley Hall* has a nominative absolute which puzzled those readers who tried to find a relation between "gleams" and "curlews."

'Tis the place, and all around it, as of old, the curlews call,
Dreary *gleams* about the moorland *flying* over Locksley Hall.

The most obvious example in current English is "weather permitting."

Nonsense Verses.—Leigh Hunt saw the possibilities of this form for the production of what Barrow called "acute nonsense," and was surprised that there were no good examples. Since he wrote, the want has been supplied by Edward Lear (see **Limerick**), and Lewis Carroll. Lear's *The Owl and the Pussy Cat* and *The Jumblies* are classics in their way, and perhaps the most triumphant of all outrages on common sense is Lewis Carroll's *Jabberwocky*. Mr. Chesterton's "A Defence of Nonsense" in *The Defendant* is admirable. None of the above have any intention to deceive, but there is a style of poem which waggish authors sometimes let loose on an uncritical public, a poem that sounds vaguely beautiful but on competent examination proves to have no sense. Mr. J. C. Squire has written one which, if it were possible, might deceive the very elect.

Novels differ from the older romances in that they depict actual everyday life. Heine says that Cervantes is the author of the modern novel, for he first introduced phases of folk-life into the romances of knighthood. In the middle of the eighteenth century Richardson, Fielding, and Smollett originated the English novel, which in the hands of their successors has become by far the most popular form of literature. Scott restored the chivalrous, aristocratic element, without neglecting the " folk-life." It is unnecessary to mention the great novelists of the nineteenth century. Here is the confession of faith made by one of them—George Meredith : " Close knowledge of our fellows, discernment of the laws of existence, these lead to great civilization. I have supposed that the novel, exposing and illustrating the natural history of man, may help us to such sustaining roadside gifts." Hazlitt had written earlier : " Good novels are the most authentic as well as most accessible repositories of the natural history and philosophy of the species." Schopenhauer on the contrary thought that the difficult task of knowing what is really going on in the world is made doubly difficult by novels ; and it is true that many novelists present us with a very unnatural history of men—and women. Even the ever delightful Dickens has probably misled readers as to the amount of promiscuous generosity floating about in the world ; and George Meredith's women, charming as they are, have been described as more like what women would wish to be than what they are. But no one would wish to exclude idealism from novels. If we wish to be tolerant, we may even endorse Poe's plea for the "fashionable" novel : " better frippery than brutality." But for the combination of brutality and unreality there is little to be said. See also **Picaresque**.

O

Octosyllabics are specifically four-foot iambic lines rhyming in couplets. (Thus they would not include the metre of Longfellow's *Hiawatha*, which is four-foot trochaic without rhyme). Chaucer used this metre in the *Romaunt of the Rose* and the *Boke of the Duchesse*, and Milton made exquisite music of it in *L'Allegro* and *Il Penseroso*, but he secured variety partly by dropping the first syllable at will. The stricter form, with an occasional feminine ending, was used with such brilliancy by Butler in *Hudibras* that " Hudibrastics " has come to be a sort of synonym for it. It was a favourite metre with the earlier eighteenth-century poets, when they wanted to get away from the heroic couplet ; Lamb delighted in Dyer's *Grongar Hill*; but, as Hartley Coleridge says, there was nothing really lyrical in the " metrical chit-chat of Prior, Lloyd, Swift, etc.—no pervading stream of music, meandering and eddying with every turn and vagary of fancy and feeling. These talkers are apt to be tiresome, if they continue long in one strain." The lyrical quality of Wordsworth's best octosyllabics is quite perfect : e.g. such lovely little poems as *Glen Almain* and *The Solitary Reaper :*

> A voice so thrilling ne'er was heard
> In spring-time from the cuckoo-bird,
> Breaking the silence of the seas,
> Among the farthest Hebrides.

Contrast the jovial vigour of Hudibras:

> For his religion, it was fit
> To match his learning and his wit.

Ode.—The ode is a **lyric** in the original sense ; the earliest odes, those of Pindar and the Greek tragedians, are incomplete without the accompaniment of music and figured dance. They are written in long-recurring stanzas called strophes, so long that the ear can hardly perceive the recurrence without the aid of repeated music and dance ; and the lines of each strophe vary in length, working in with the accompaniments. Anacreon's odes are different, written in short lines without strophes. There is also the ode in short stanzas, of which Horace supplies the best-known examples; but he had his Greek models—Sappho, Alcæus, etc. English odes start with Drayton. He followed Horace and Anacreon, " but he was chiefly haunted," says Professor Elton, " by the loud and sharp accompaniment of the Irish or British harp ; and its twangle, its

ODE

decisive note, passed into the loudest of his verses." The *Ballad of Agincourt* is well known, and here is a charming stanza from the ode *To the New Year*:

> Give her th' Eoan brightness
> Wing'd with that subtle lightness
>   That doth transpierce the air;
> The roses of the morning
> The rising heaven adorning
>   To mesh with flames of hair.

The tone of sustained rapture, which is essential to the idea of the ode, is loud in Shelley's *Skylark*. The **Pindaric** ode was attempted by Ben Jonson—the well-known lines—

> It is not growing like a tree
> In bulk, doth make men better be,

occur in one; made fashionable by Cowley; twice achieved with great art and magnificence by Gray; and written with doubtful success by Wordsworth and Shelley. Even in the great *Intimations of Immortality* the irregularity of form is not always felt to justify itself. Keats's consummate odes are written in regular stanzas; Stopford Brooke doubtfully excepts them from his judgment that the ode is the least satisfactory of lyric forms: "Nearly all odes have the air of being schemed beforehand, even of being written to order; the form of the ode seems to suggest these faults." Pindar's odes were undoubtedly written to order, and are thereby the more miraculous. So was Dryden's *Alexander's Feast*. Perhaps the traditional requirement of " rapture " tends to make the writer self-conscious ; certainly the supposed " irregularity " of Pindar is a mere stumbling-block to writers who have not his aids. See also **Pindaric.**

Onomatopœia in its first sense is simply name-making, with special reference to the Stoic theory that words are formed to suggest by their sound the idea presented. In Latin they could point to *lenis*, smooth ; *asper*, rough ; *lana*, wool ; *vepres*, briar ; etc., etc. So far, however, is this principle—the bow-wow theory, as Max Müller nicknamed it—from being " the very cradle of language," that it accounts for comparatively few words : e.g. bang, cuckoo, twitter. But as applied to the choice of words in poetry, whereby the sound is made " an echo to the sense," onomatopœia has a real existence. The most obvious examples are those in which the sense to be echoed is itself a sound : e.g. two knights in armour " shocked, like an iron-clanging anvil banged with hammers " (Tennyson).

Doves of the fir-wood walling high our red roof
Through the long noon coo, crooning through the coo
   (Meredith)

ONOMATOPŒIA

Fountains, and ye that warble as ye flow,
Melodious murmurs, warbling tune His praise (Milton).

Even Johnson, who was sceptical in the matter, admitted the effectiveness of the last example. Motion may be "echoed" by extra short syllables, consecutive long syllables, cross-rhythms, strong pauses, etc.: e.g.

Myriads of rivulets hurrying through the lawn—

First, as in fear, step after step, she stole,
Down the long tower-stairs, hesitating—

As on a dull day in an ocean cave
The blind wave feeling round his long sea-hall
In silence (Tennyson)

The strong-built pillars of his soul, that stood
Steady, though in the slippery paths of blood
(Chamberlayne).

But this sort of thing may easily become too ingenious to fit easily with the context, and then it gives the effect of a mere trick. And anyone can collect words containing s to describe a snake, or words beginning with h to describe a laborious effort. The best use of onomatopœia needs a much subtler art, and pervades the description in a way which satisfies without surprising the ear. Dryden's *Alexander's Feast* and Tennyson's *Lotus Eaters* are obvious examples of the way in which metre may be made to suit the sense.

Oxymoron (pointedly foolish) is a combination of contrary ideas, a phrase seemingly absurd but really significant : e.g. the jarring harmony of nature, strenuous idleness, masterly inactivity, timidly firm. Byron says that human affairs are " prolific of melancholy merriment," and ascribes to St. Peter's " gigantic elegance." Bentley wrote of " the pitiless mercies, the salutary torments of a popish inquisition." Spenser's " proud humility " is a beautiful example. It is very frequent in Sidney's *Arcadia*. Meredith in *Night of Frost in May* writes " in this shrill hush of quietude."

P

Parable is a short allegory. The term is specially used of the tales told by Christ for the sake of instruction, and has therefore a more serious meaning than **fable**; it would not include animal stories. Jotham's so-called parable about the trees choosing a king is rather a fable or **apologue**; whereas Nathan's rebuke to David is more similar to the Gospel parables. A parable and an apologue both remind us of the occasion on which they were delivered; allegories and fables are chiefly thought of as literature.

Paradox is a statement seemingly absurd but really true: e.g. Whose service is perfect freedom: that which thou sowest is not quickened except it die. Its object is to gain attention, which it easily does, says Johnson, " when recommended by spirit and elegance." Otherwise it fails, as a line in one of Dryden's plays failed in performance, and caused the play to fail too. The actress, having pathetically declared " My wound is great, because it is so small ! " paused and looked distressed. Whereupon the Duke of Buckingham jumped up and added in a loud voice—" Then 'twould be greater were it none at all," which effectually quenched the poor lady. Yet there may be truth in the notion : the pettiness of an injury may increase the vexation caused by it ; but the word "small" in Dryden's line is unfortunately ambiguous. George Meredith's powerful statesmen, checked by aristocratic exclusiveness, "gnawed the paradox that it [the opposition] was huge because it was petty." For examples of paradox see Mr. G. K. Chesterton's prose works *passim*.

Parody or travesty is an imitation, usually of a serious work, meant to excite laughter at its expense. Byron's *Vision of Judgment* is a parody of Southey, and is one of the very few examples which are also good in themselves. The *Rejected Addresses* contain admirable parodies, especially those of Crabbe, Scott, and Wordsworth. Canning's *Loves of the Triangles* is a very brilliant travesty of Erasmus Darwin's *Loves of the Plants*, and may still be read with pleasure though the work which provoked it is probably the most inanimate corpse in the graveyard of great reputations. A good parody may be a valuable indirect criticism. Calverley's on *The Ring and the Book* is masterly. See also **Pastiche.**

Paronomasia is a long name for a pun, a play on words. Its literary use dates at least

PARONOMASIA

from Æschylus. Shakespeare, says Hazlitt, was fonder of puns than became so great a man. This deplorable fact may be partly due to the fashion of his times—Marlowe writes " hell and darkness pitch their pitchy tents "—partly to the exuberant activity of his mind ; but Coleridge has made a good case for the pun as the language of suppressed passion. " A passion there is that carries off its own excess by plays on words as naturally —and therefore as appropriately to drama— as by gesticulation, looks, or tones." It is also the language of contemptuous exultation. When Milton's Satan addressed his troops before firing his guns—a species of frightfulness till then unknown—he punned in a devilish manner ; and after the confusion caused in the angelic ranks by the discharge, Belial did likewise. But it is sad to find Raphael, in telling the tale to Adam, condescend to the same figure of speech ; and it is clear from other places that Milton rather liked a pun : e.g. which tempted our attempt : at one slight bound high overleaped all bound (of Satan getting over the garden wall) : beseeching or besieging : their armour helped their harm—a rather Cockney pun. Swift and Macaulay delighted in the private use of the pun, and Charles Lamb encouraged it both by precept and example. The contemptuous intention is clear in Gibbon's description of two forms of penance as " these compensations of the purse and the person." There has been much unthinking abuse of the pun, in both senses of " abuse "—vituperation and wrong use. " The seeds of punning," says Addison, " are in the minds of all men," and it does seem rather inhuman to be shocked by the indulgence of an instinct so universal.

Particles are the short connecting words of language, more plentiful in the modern than in the classical tongues, owing to our loss of case- and tense-forms. Sylvester relates how Adam first invented his nouns and verbs:

> And then, the more t' enrich his speech, he brings
> Small particles, which stand in lieu of strings,
> The master members fitly to combine,
> As two great boards a little glue doth join.

So Coleridge speaks of the conjunctions which link the clauses of a period as " the cements of language." Miss Seward is more contemptuous. She praises that manner of the eighteenth-century writers which " sweeps from the polished marble of poetry and eloquence a number of the sticks and straws of our language: its articles, conjunctions and prepositions." Those writers, aiming at the terse and weighty idiom of Latin, found an obstacle in the multitude of our particles, and laboured to dispense with them. Dryden sadly admits that we cannot be so concise: "We and all the modern tongues have more articles and pronouns, besides signs of tenses and cases, and other barbarities on which our speech is built, by the faults of our forefathers." He was fond of Sylvester in his youth, so he must have known that Adam was the original criminal.

Pastiche is said to mean a hotch-potch or medley. It is used of pictures which are neither originals nor copies, but put together from various existing pictures. However, in literature a pastiche is a study in discipleship which has no intention to ridicule, and is therefore not a parody. Burke's early work, *A Vindication of Natural Society*, was so close an imitation of Bolingbroke's style that it deceived such good judges as Lord Chesterfield and Bishop Warburton, and failed in its ironical intention. A pastiche is a deliberate imitation, and the term would not apply to works written under the more or less unconscious influence of a great writer such as Spenser, Pope, or Tennyson. Wordsworth's Stanzas in imitation of Thomson's *Castle of Indolence* would be a fair example. So is Meredith's *The Shaving of Shagpat*, modelled on *The Arabian Nights*.

Pastoral Poetry is properly that which deals with the life of shepherds and rustics generally. See **Idyll.** But Bion in his lament for Moschus, presented that poet under the guise of a shepherd, and Virgil did the same sort of thing in his **Bucolics.** Hence grew up the strange convention of writing about all sorts of persons as if they were shepherds and led a pastoral life. It is easy to ridicule the practice. Johnson's common sense revolted against it, and certainly such a spectacle as the melancholic landscape-gardener Shenstone warbling about his crook, his pipe, and his kids provokes mirth. But the fact remains that some of the loveliest of English poems were written according to this convention, and we must accept the convention or lose great pleasure. Milton's *Lycidas*, Shelley's *Adonais*, and Arnold's *Thyrsis* more than justify it. " There is grace ineffable, a sweet sound and sweet savour of things past, in the old beautiful use of the language of shepherds, of flocks and pipes ; the spirit is none the less sad and sincere because the body of the poem has put on this dear familiar raiment of romance ; because the crude and naked sorrow is veiled and chastened with soft shadows of a 'land that is very far off'" (Swinburne). Spenser's pastorals, though composed " mainly for the purposes of metrical

PASTORAL POETRY—PATHETIC FALLACY

experiment," are written with sincerity and charm, but Pope's early *Pastorals* are merely a vapid exhibition of smooth versification. The content of the pastoral was further enlarged, and its motive complicated, by the introduction of satire under the veil of allegory. The Italian Mantuan and the French Marot led Spenser along this by-road; and Milton followed the same course in the bitter attack on the clergy which startles us in *Lycidas*. There are also Pastoral Romances such as Sidney's *Arcadia*, in which, however, the romantic element almost entirely overshadows the pastoral; and Pastoral Dramas such as Fletcher's *Faithful Shepherdess*. "Perhaps the best pastoral in the language," says Hazlitt, "is that prose-poem, Walton's *Compleat Angler*"; and Burke held that Goldsmith's *Deserted Village* beat not only Pope but Spenser also, in that style.

Pathetic fallacy is a phrase coined by Ruskin to denote that falseness in our impressions of external objects which is due to emotion: more shortly, illusion due to passion. The commonest form is seen in the tendency of poets and impassioned writers generally to ascribe human feelings to inanimate nature at large. Leigh Hunt reckoned this tendency as one of the constituent parts of the poetic imagination, and noticed how the

Greek pastoral poets made floods and flowers sympathize with human woe. Their modern imitators have eagerly followed the lead; Sidney's *Arcadia* abounds with examples, some think to excess; "he is for ever hearing tongues in trees" is the impatient remark of a modern critic. Clearly the thing may be overdone, and become a **conceit.** Tennyson held that Wordsworth was justified in saying that the moon looked round her with delight when the heavens were bare, but that another poet went too far when he called the wave " a bride wooing the shore." Nor did he like Kingsley's " cruel, crawling wave " (for " foam "), as too much like a live creature. If we place it beside Milton's " remorseless deep," it does seem rather neurotic ; or we might call it the feminine of Milton's masculine phrase. Tennyson's own famous lines—

> As on a dull day in an ocean cave
> The blind wave feeling round his long sea-hall
> In silence—

might to some suggest Polyphemus, but we must suppose they did not to the author.

Pause is a stoppage in the flow of verse. It occurs *more or less* at the end of every line, but pauses within the line are one great element in the various music of verse. Abbott and Seeley in their admirable paragraphs on the pause quote this example of Milton's variety in its use :

From branch to branch the smaller birds with songs
Solaced the woods,|and spread their painted wings,
Till even ;|nor then the solemn nightingale
Ceased warbling,|but all night tuned her soft lays.|
Others,|in silver lakes and rivers,|bathed
Their downy breast ;|the swan, with archèd neck
Between her white wings mantling proudly,|rows
Her state with oary feet ;|yet oft they quit
The dank,|and rising on swift pennons,|tower
The mid aerial sky.|Others on ground
Walked firm :|the crested cock whose clarion sounds
The silent hours,|and the other whose gay train
Adorns him,|coloured with the florid hue
Of rainbows and starry eyes.

See also **Cæsura, Enjambment.**

Pedantesque.—See under **Macaronic.**

Pegasus was a winged horse of Greek mythology. At a stroke of his hoof the fountain Hippocrene (horse-fount) gushed forth on Mount Helicon ; and as that was the haunt of the **Muses,** the Renaissance poets adopted Pegasus as the Muses' steed and a symbol of the poet's soaring genius. Modern references are usually more or less jocose. It has been said of Campbell that " the springs of his Helicon were neither frequent nor full, and it required a special stamp of one breed of Pegasus to set them flowing." Of an uninspired poet Byron wrote " he spurs his jaded Pegasus apace." Shortly after Shelley's death the *Gentleman's Magazine* stated that he " published certain convulsive caperings of Pegasus labouring under cholic pains."

Pentameter is a line of five feet, especially the sort used by Greeks and Romans to make, alternately with the **hexameter,** their elegiac couplet. Coleridge has both described and imitated this couplet—

In the hex|ámeter|ríses the|foúntaín's|sílvery|cólumn,
In the pen|támeter|aye||fálling in|mélody|back.

Tennyson expressed his dislike of English hexameters in six such couplets : e.g.

Was there a|harsher|sound ever|heard, ye|Muses, in| England ?
When did a|frog coars|er||croak upon|our Heli|con ?

He also produced this disrespectful pentameter : " All men alike hate slops, particularly gruel."

Period is a sentence consisting of several clauses which are so arranged that the sense is not finished till the close. This is very effective in oratory. Bulwer Lytton thus describes Pitt's method :

We hear the elaborate swell of that full strain
Linking long periods in completest chain ;
Staying the sense, from sentence sentence grows,
Till the last word comes clinching up the close.

Hooker's written style was periodic, "long and pithy," says Fuller, "driving on a whole flock of several clauses before he came to the close of a sentence." Bain quotes a masterly specimen: " On the whole, while the *Essay on Criticism* [Pope's] may be readily allowed to be superior in execution, as it is certainly in compass, to any work of a similar nature in English poetry, it can hardly be said either to redeem the class of didactic poems on æsthetics from the neglect into which they have fallen, or to make us regret that the critical ability of our own day should prefer to follow the path marked out by Dryden when he chose to discourse of poetry in his own vigorous and flexible prose." Such sentences compel us to read with close attention, and impress us with the writer's power; in good hands they may achieve wonders of rhythm and climax, but short sentences like Macaulay's are clearer and more immediately effective. M. Taine goes so far as to say that one true phrase is worth a hundred periods, which indeed French style does not affect. In this matter, as in others, variety is best. Abbott and Seeley notice how often Burke prefixes to a long rhetorical sentence " a kind of introductory epitome of what is going to be said."

Periphrasis consists in expressing the meaning of a word, phrase, etc., by many or several words instead of by few or one (*N.E.D.*) : e.g. the cup that cheers but not inebriates = tea. Pindar calls a cloak " the warm antidote of cold winds." In good writing there is no such thing as a " mere periphrasis " ; the words used will always convey ideas which the writer wishes to add to the simple conception. When Milton calls clothes " those troublesome disguises which we wear," he is not simply filling out a line, but suggesting a perfectly appropriate aspect of clothes. Tennyson's phrase for mathematics, " the hard-grained Muses of the cube and square," vividly indicates his attitude towards that branch of study. But when for " grey beard " he writes " the many-wintered fleece of throat and chin," the hubbub of words— to use Johnson's phrase—seems excessive. Wordsworth too often sins in this way : e.g. the street that from Oxford has borrowed its name : that rose which from the prime derives its name : the fragrant beverage drawn from China's herb. Oxford-street, primrose, and tea are no-wise adorned by these periphrases. Indeed the figure is often used with comic intention, and Lamb is particularly fond of it : e.g. the blue-aproned contunder of the calf=butcher. Shenstone in an admirable Miltonic parody calls pins " the cure of rents and separations dire, and chasms enormous." But in less skilful hands this sort of thing becomes wearisome or offensive. There is—or was—a dismal version of *The House that Jack built*, beginning "This is the domiciliary edifice erected by John," and so on. Shakespeare will write a periphrasis out of "a sort of fulness of heart, parallel to that which makes the merry boy whistle as he walks" (Newman): e.g. with taper light to seek the beauteous eye of heaven to garnish=to hold a candle to the sun.

Personification is the creation of a fictitious person in order to account for (1) psychological, (2) obscure physical phenomena (Abbott and Seeley); i.e. the presentation of our own feelings, or facts of the outer world, as persons: e.g. Hope told a flattering tale: the winds are all asleep. Lord Orrery says of Pope: "Pleasure dwelt under his roof, and Elegance presided at his table." This tendency to assign a personal existence to all forms of activity is a perpetual instinct of the mind; in this as in other ways the poet feels the impulse of the savage and the child. Shelley's poem *The Cloud* is one long personification. Abstract qualities are continually personified by the poets, to make their operation more vivid. Virgil's elaborate picture of Rumour has had many imitators.

In Milton's lovely description of evening with the nightingales' song, the words "Silence was pleased" have a wonderful if nameless charm; and there is something very memorable in Keats's picture of "Joy, whose hand is ever at his lips bidding adieu." But the figure has been much abused. Unless the personified quality does something characteristic, the mere spelling with a capital letter—"printer's devil's personifications" is Coleridge's phrase—contributes nothing to the vividness of the picture. Erasmus Darwin congratulates the English language on possessing two great aids to the achievement of a figure in which he wallowed—the use of masculine or feminine pronouns and the omission of the article! Wordsworth deliberately avoided the promiscuous use of the figure, though he allowed it as occasionally prompted by passion. There is a goodly crew —Labour, Hope, etc.—near the end of the third book of *The Prelude*.

Picaresque means relating to rogues. A form of novel with a rogue for hero was invented in Spain, when it was the land of adventurers, and copied under Elizabeth, especially by Thomas Nash. The hero is "faithless, shameless, if not joyless, the plaything of fortune, by turns valet, gentleman, courtier, thief. We follow him in all societies." The only drawback is that this hero "has necessarily little conscience and still less heart" (Jusserand). This sort of tale supplied the comic element almost entirely lacking in such popular romances as *Arcadia*, and had a success which the later development of the novel has almost completely obscured. Defoe worked the same vein in his *Life and Piracies of Captain Singleton*, and *Life and Adventures of Colonel Jack*, with a realism greatly enhanced; and some of the novels of Smollett and Thackeray belong to the class.

Pindaric Ode.—At the time when the strict heroic couplet was establishing its tyranny over English metre, there came a reaction in favour of freer measures written under a mistaken notion of Pindar's method (see **Ode**). Complete irregularity in the length of the lines and of the long sections, sudden digressions and bold figures—out of these ingredients and his own sound learning and wit Cowley constructed a number of odes which were highly praised at the time and much imitated by his successors. But Cowley, though his learning and his fertile fancy make him an interesting writer, completely lacked two qualities necessary to the poet—strong feeling and a sense of the magic of words. His imitators are quite unreadable.

The death of Charles II produced a torrent of "Pindaricks," but not even Dryden's contribution, *Threnodia Augustalis*, pleases now. However, his *Alexander's Feast* is a wonderful *tour-de-force* in this unpromising style. Congreve saw that mere irregularity can never be a successful principle of versification, and restored the strophic structure of Pindar. Gray's *Progress of Poesy* and *The Bard* observe the same method, but their undoubted majesty owes little if anything to the recurrence of the measures. Gray's earlier opinion was that the ear could not hold a stanza of more than nine lines, Spenser's number, so as to feel pleasure in the repetition. The Pindaric ode is now quite dead. It is significant that the period of its vogue was precisely the period when English poets seem to have lost the secret of writing real lyrics.

Plagiarism is "cribbing," appropriating the phrases and ideas of other writers. "Borrowing," says Milton, "if it be not bettered by the borrower, among good authors is accounted plagiarie." It is useless to discuss the morality of the practice. Writers have always copied each other, whether consciously or unconsciously, and will always do so. "This partnership and community of goods has always been allowed to poets and other writers," says the Roman critic. We condemn them only if they spoil what they borrow. "The Spartan law holds good in literature, where to steal is honourable, provided it be done with skill and dexterity: wherefore Mercury was the patron both of thieves and poets" (F. Thompson). Some plagiarism undoubtedly strikes us as mean, but to give good reasons for our feeling is not easy. Poets differ considerably in the extent of their thefts; few have stolen so continually and skilfully as Gray, whose poems are mosaics put together from fragments of previous writers—the method of modern writers of Latin verse. Some feel cheated when they find an "original" poem so composed; to others the recognition of known jewels in a new setting is an extra pleasure. There is no question of saving trouble, in the borrowings of a true poet. If anyone thinks it an easy matter to make memorable poetry out of other men's phrases, let him just try. But we are more grateful to the maker of a fine phrase than we are to a skilful stealer. Molière, Sterne, Dumas and Disraeli are among the mighty plagiarists.

Pleonasm, or **tautology,** consists in adding words not necessary for the sense. Puttenham's example is "I heard it with mine ears and saw it with mine eyes—as if a man could hear with his heels or see with his nose." It may be a legitimate means of emphasis: e.g. swim or sink, live or die, survive or perish with my country. An interesting form of tautology became fashionable in the sixteenth and seventeenth centuries to explain a foreign-derived word by its native equivalent. Caxton has "to build and edify their habitation and dwelling." It is frequent in the *Book of Common Prayer*; e.g. we have erred and strayed from Thy ways. Bacon has "He breatheth and inspireth light into the face of His chosen." There are some surprising examples of the figure in Milton: e.g. a globe of circular light. Coleridge remarks that " passion, inducing in the mind an unusual activity, seeks for means to waste its superfluity, in lyric repetitions and sublime tautology." He quotes from the song of Deborah: "At her feet he bowed, he fell, he lay down; at her feet he bowed, he fell; where he bowed, there he fell down dead" (see **Repetition**). Here are examples of the abuse of tautology: break through the billows and divide the main: in smoother numbers and in softer verse: and now and then a tear stole down by stealth (Byron). Bain distinguishes between tautology and pleonasm, the first adding a superfluous word or words in the same grammatical place, pleonasm repeating the meaning in a different place.

Poetic Licence.—If by this phrase—" that shrewd fellow," Gascoigne calls it—we mean that a poet has full liberty to write differently from a prose writer, there is perhaps no harm in it, and not much good. Goldsmith applies it to such phrases as cruel sword, ruffian blast, faithful bosom of earth, because they would not be used in prose. If we mean by it that a poet is not to be condemned for bad pronunciation, bad grammar, or bad taste, it is simply false, " a phrase which has to answer for an infinity of sins " (Poe). Here the judicious Quintilian for once fails us. " Poets, he says, " being slaves to their metre, are pardoned for their faults by giving names to them ; we call them metaplasms and schematisms, and praise as a virtue what was really a necessity." But the alleged necessity simply does not arise. The poet is the master and not the slave of his metre. He has at command dozens of different ways of saying what he wants to say, and chooses that way which best expresses the full content of his thought. It is no licence to choose a less usual form of expression if that form best gives the impression desired. Chapman protested against " that most vulgar and foolish receipt of poetic licence, being of all knowing men to be exploded." Roscommon says that it "belongs to none but an establish'd fame, which scorns to take it." And Mr. Austin Dobson quotes an eloquent protest by M. Théodore de Banville (*A Bookman's Budget*, 125).

Poetry, Forms of.—Wordsworth enumerates six main forms: (1) Narrative, including Epic; (2) Dramatic; (3) Lyric; (4) Idyllic, in which he includes such descriptive poems as Thomson's *Seasons*, Shenstone's *Schoolmistress*, Burns's *The Cottar's Saturday Night*, Milton's *L'Allegro* and *Il Penseroso*, Goldsmith's *Deserted Village*; (5) Didactic; (6) Philosophical Satire, like that of Horace and Juvenal; personal and occasional Satire rarely comprehending sufficient of the general in the individual to be dignified with the name of poetry. Out of the last three, he adds, has been constructed a composite order, of which Young's *Night Thoughts* and Cowper's *Task* are excellent examples.

Precious, ever since Molière, has been used to describe affectation of refinement, whether in manners or in style. It is rather precious of Tennyson to describe Arthur's moustache as "the knightly growth that fringed his lip," to say nothing of the unfortunate ambiguity to a hearer. Where there is conspicuous refinement of style, as in Pater,

Stevenson, and Mrs. Meynell, the enemy will always infer affectation, and call the style precious. When the refinement bears evident traces of the effort by which it was attained, the censure is just; the style distracts our attention from the matter; that highest art which conceals art is lacking. But the word "affectation" begs the question. When a style deliberately adopted has become the writer's natural mode of expression, it is rather unfair to call it affected. Sometimes the word "precious" is used without the notion of censure, meaning just fastidious in the use of words.

Pre-Raphaelitism was first the artistic creed of certain painters, who about 1850 formed the Pre-Raphaelite Brotherhood. It was a protest against the generalizing methods of Raphael, and even more against their feeble imitation by later painters. It insisted on truth and accuracy of detail as the foundation of all strength and beauty in art. A similar protest, concerning literary methods, had been made fifty years earlier by Wordsworth and the **romantic** poets; and even before them Crabbe had shown how strength—but not in his case beauty—relies on detail. The difficulty is how to work in the details so that they shall not distract attention from the whole, but rather contribute to its rich unity. Wordsworth sometimes overdid his detail, but had the good sense to listen to criticism. In *The Thorn*, describing a wayside puddle, he crowns his stanza with this glowing couplet:

> I've measured it from side to side;
> 'Tis two feet long and three feet wide.

But this disappeared on later revision. In *The Ancient Mariner* Coleridge originally wrote, of the albatross, "The mariners gave it biscuit worms," as no doubt they did; but feeling the undue emphasis of a detail so striking, he altered the line to the more **general** but more imaginative, form—"It ate the food it ne'er had ate."

Prolepsis is the anticipative use of an adjective: e.g. the lazy nurse who snores the sick man *dead*: to strain a liquid *clear*, i.e. so as to become clear. This form of prolepsis, with the adjective following the noun, is quite common. Less obvious, but fairly frequent, are such examples as: to make the mountain quarries move, and call the *walking* woods (Ben Jonson): nor bound thy *narrow* views to things below (Pope): shall strike his *aching* breast against a post (Gay): to scatter plenty o'er a *smiling* land (Gray): and furls his *wrinkly* front (Shenstone): patience, sovereign o'er *transmuted* ill (John-

PROLEPSIS—PYRRHIC

son): huge oaks stalk down the *unshaded* mountain's side (Young): a wandering stream of wind ... has caught the *expanded* sail (Shelley). A probably unique instance is Keats's " So the two brothers and their *murdered* man Rode past fair Florence," where the proleptic adjective forms no part of the verbal notion.

Pyrrhic is a two-syllable foot with no strong accent: e.g. but fooled with hope, men fa|vour the|deceit (Dryden): that se|cret to| each fool, that he's an ass (Pope): oh weep for Adona|is! the|quick dreams (Shelley). Notice in the last three examples, how a spondee close by compensates the weak pyrrhic. This is characteristic of Milton's versification:

> Say first—for heaven hides no|thing from|thy view,
> Nor the|deep tract of hell—say first what cause
> Moved our grand pa|rents in|that happy state.

Professor Mayor admits the pyrrhic in his analysis of English verse, but some prosodists regard a foot without an accent as a contradiction in terms. See **Scansion.**

Q

Quantity.—In Greek and Latin prosody syllables are classed as either long or short, according to the time taken in pronouncing them; feet (see **Foot**) are defined as arrangements of long and short syllables, not, as in English, of syllables accented and unaccented; the nature of a syllable from this point of view is called its quantity. **Accent** being the determining force in English metre, the influence of quantity is sometimes overlooked, but it sensibly affects the rhythm. Though "city" and "charming" are both trochees, their time value is different; the first syllable of one being short, of the other long. Even in unaccented syllables, quantity counts. In Latin a word like "resplendent" would consist of three longs; in English the strong accent on the middle syllable tends to shorten the other two, but they are clearly not so short as in e.g. "related"; and these considerations affect the sound, and therefore the emotional character, of all English verse. Dryden and Cowper went so far as to say that they found every syllable as clearly long or short in English as in Latin or Greek; and

Tennyson knew the quantities of every English word, except perhaps "scissors"; but nobody has been able to write down the rules. Tennyson wrote some extremely interesting imitations of Latin metres "in quantity," which deserve careful study. See also Mr. Mallock's lines quoted at the end of the article **Hexameter.** Though a strong accent will always obscure quantity, the strength of the accent will vary in the speech of different ages, and there is some reason to think that English pronunciation is now more quantitative than it was. Yet we do not notice much improvement in the shockingly indistinct articulation of most English people.

Quatrain is a **stanza** of four lines.

R

Refrain or burden is a word or set of words recurring usually after each stanza, sometimes within the stanza. It was common in the old ballads, being taken up by the whole throng, after the lines allotted to individuals. It naturally occurs in lullabies, as "Balow, my babe, lie still and sleep." Tennyson's *Oriana* is an early modern example, and Mangan made fine play with his " Karaman, O Karaman." The refrain with variety contributes to the memorable effect of Poe's *The Raven*. Mrs. Browning used the burden "Toll slowly" to set the key, as it were, to her *Rhyme of the Duchess May;* Rossetti's *Sister Helen* weaves a continual refrain, as a sort of steadying influence, in the web of its passionate story; William Morris's "Two red roses across the moon" illustrates the quasi-hypnotic effect of mere repetition with no particular meaning. The primitive pleasure found in repetition, on which the charm of rhythm and of rhyme is based, finds a striking illustration in the effectiveness of the refrain. But it does not always " come off." Calverley was justified

REPETITION

in poking fun at Jean Ingelow's "O love my Willie!"

Repetition is a powerful weapon of the orator; it is indeed an essential element in persuasive speech. Its value is not unknown to writers in the daily press, whether admirals or not. Matthew Arnold in his prose repeated certain phrases with such determination that they became national property. In poetry repetition (anaphora, epanaphora) may be used thus, for emphasis: e.g. Churchill's satirical lines on Scotland:

> Thence simple bards, by simple prudence taught,
> To this wise town by simple patrons brought,
> In simple manner utter simple lays,
> And take, with simple pensions, simple praise.

In particular, it may emphasize the continuity of an action, as in Sylvester's description of the Flood overtaking those who fled from it—

> And still—still mounting as they still do mount,
> When they cease mounting, doth them soon surmount.

This is not very charming, but the intention is the same as in Shelley's fine line about the lark, which "singing still dost soar, and soaring ever singest." When variety is added to the repetition, it may be very effective, as in Milton's—

> To love bondage more than liberty,
> Bondage with ease than strenuous liberty.

REPETITION

Wordsworth is very fond of this locution: e.g.

> The boundaries of space and time,
> Of melancholy space and doleful time.

And again—

> Calm did he sit under the wide-spread tree
> Of his old age: and yet less calm and meek,
> Winningly meek or venerably calm,
> Than slow and torpid.

Dryden several times notices the beauty of these "turns on words" as he calls them. They were much practised by Spenser and the other Elizabethans, but neglected by the poets of Dryden's day, except the veteran Milton. There is a long example of great beauty in Eve's address to Adam (*Paradise Lost*, iv, ll. 641–56), in which the repetitions are sufficiently far apart to avoid the mechanical effect noticeable in some of the Elizabethan writers. Repetition for the sake of pathos is universal in language. A famous example is David's lament: "O my son Absalom, my son, my son Absalom! would God I had died for thee, O Absalom, my son, my son!" The poetic prose of Sidney's *Arcadia* supplies another: "'My Argalus! my Argalus!' said she, 'do not thus forsake me. Remember, alas! remember that I have interest in you which I will never yield shall thus be adventured. Your valour is already sufficiently known, sufficient have you already done for your country; enow, enow there are beside you to lose less worthy lives.' "

Rhetoric is in the first place the art of persuading by speech; then it is used of eloquent speech or writing. As we are more easily persuaded by appeal to our passions and sympathies than by arguments addressed to the reason, "rhetorical" has acquired a depreciatory sense, and is opposed to "logical." Rhetoric aims at a practical result, not the investigation of abstract truth. As applied to poetry the scope of the word "rhetorical" is more difficult to fix. It may mean "artificial" or even "ostentatious," and suggest the insincerity of the emotions it embodies or endeavours to excite. "The art of making great matters small, and small things great" is the definition of Isocrates, himself a great rhetorician. But poetry is not always concerned with our deepest feelings; especially in description its business may be, as De Quincey says, "to aggrandize and bring out into strong relief, by means of various and striking thoughts, some aspect of truth which by itself is supported by no spontaneous feelings, and therefore rests upon artificial aid." The elaborate speeches delivered by messengers in Greek tragedy are a good example, so different is their style from the Attic simplicity of the other dialogue. Chapman has imitated them in the account of a fight in *Bussy d'Amboise*. The success of the rhetoric depends on its effectiveness in exciting those less active feelings of which De Quincey speaks. " Rhetoric is very good, or stark naught," says Selden. Here is an example of Milton's gorgeous rhetoric :

> Attended with ten thousand thousand saints,
> He onward came ; far off His coming shone ;
> And twenty thousand (I their number heard)
> Chariots of God, half on each hand, were seen.
> He on the wings of Cherub rode sublime
> On the crystalline sky, in sapphire throned,—
> Illustrious far and wide, but by His own
> First seen.

Rhyme is normally concerned with the final accented syllables of two or more lines. When the vowel sounds of these, with the following consonants, are identical, the lines are said to rhyme. When the ending is **feminine,** the final (unaccented) syllable must also be identical : e.g. goose, loose ; together, weather. Rhyme is so usual an element of modern poetry that **blank verse** is so named as exceptional, but it was unknown to classical Latin and Greek. It is " a main source to our poetry of its magic and charm " (Arnold) ; the jingle which pleases the child and the

RHYME

barbarian may be so varied as to give a high sensuous pleasure ; and so far from distracting us from the thought, it may supply to the thought its most effective expression. It reinforces the great effect of metre, satisfying our craving for identity in variety, providing another limitation, giving the streams of passion " banks within which to flow, if they are not to waste and lose themselves altogether." We often hear of the fetters of rhyme, but Scott is right : " Rhyme, which is a handcuff to an inferior poet, he who is master of his art wears as a bracelet." Undoubtedly rhyme is sometimes master and suggests a thought, as Dryden candidly admitted. When Browning wrote—

> So, the storm subsides to calm :
> They see the green trees wave
> On the heights o'erlooking Grève.
> Hearts that bled are staunched with balm—

the last line is obviously influenced by the necessity of rhyming. Browning is full of such *tours de force*—he once found a rhyme for " rhinoceros " ;—but they are more witty than poetical as a rule. In Wordsworth they are sometimes very flat : e.g.

> So the shaft
> Of victory mounts high, and blood is quaffed (!)
> In fields that rival Cressy and Poictiers—
> Pride to be washed away by bitter tears !

When the rhyme word is an important one, it gains additional emphasis from the rhyme; but then there is a danger of breaking the natural flow of the verse, and writing in epigrams, as Pope often does. The principle of variety requires the occasional use of unemphatic rhymes: e.g.

> Haste thee, nymph, and bring with thee
> Jest and youthful Jollity.

Some varieties of rhyme deserve notice: (1) internal rhyme, common in ballad metres: e.g.

> We were the first that ever burst
> Into that silent sea—

and used in odd places by Poe in *The Raven* and elsewhere: (2) *rime riche*, a feature of French and Italian poetry, when the initial consonants of the rhyme syllables are identical as well as the rest; Milton rhymes the name Ruth with the common noun; it is frequent in Spenser, and see the lines of Wordsworth quoted above: (3) double or feminine rhyme —e.g. tender, slender—which Dryden considered a part of burlesque writing; but he used it himself in an epitaph, and it is quite frequent in our best poetry: (4) triple rhyme —e.g. Send him victorious, Happy and glorious—which needs much tact if it is not to give a burlesque effect ; Hood has succeeded in *The Bridge of Sighs*. The use of rhyme in poetic drama has been a matter of fierce dispute. It is noteworthy that Shakespeare used it less in his later plays. Not even Dryden's genius could make it a success. But in French tragedy it is the rule. As M. Taine says : " Rhyme is a different thing in different races. To an Englishman it resembles a song, and transports him at once to an ideal and fairy world. To a Frenchman it is only a conventionalism or an expediency, and transports him at once to an antechamber or a drawing-room ; to him it is an ornamental dress and nothing more." Perhaps it is impossible for us to realize why a drawing-room gives the most suitable atmosphere for tragedy. Rhyme without metre has been used with comic effect by Swift—*Mrs. Harris's Petition*, Hood—*Our Village* and *A Charity Sermon*, Gilbert—*Lost Mr. Blake*, and by Southey in a letter : " We took such excellent care of our baggage, that we have great reason to be *glad*—having lost nothing but my old great-coat, and a bundle of linen in its pockets, and Edith's new green *plaid*."

Rhythm in words is due to a more or less regular recurrence of emphasis ; its effect is to embody and convey emotion. " It is an enrapturer of the poet, exalts him as a creator, and augments all his powers " (Darley). " Rhythm is not a thing invented by man, but a thing evolved from him " (Lewes). " All deep and sustained feeling has tended to express itself in rhythmical language " (Mill). The oratory of savages is a good example. Thus the arrangement of words and sentences which produces the rhythm is no convention, but responds to a genuine need of the soul. When the recurrence of the emphasis is regular, or approximates recognizably to a regular form, the words are divisible into feet and lines, and we get metre, but in good verse the metre is never so monotonously regular as to forbid varieties of rhythm ; the metrical scheme sets a standard, variations of accent and quantity diversify the rhythm. As Dr. Johnson says, the metrical rule must be " lax enough to substitute similitude for identity, to admit change without breach of order, and to relieve the ear without disappointing it." Here are two lines from Tennyson, both blank verse, but very different in effect—

The long day wanes, the slow moon climbs, the deep—
Immingled with heaven's azure waveringly.

These are extreme instances, but the ever-present efficacy of rhythm is shown by the fact that different poets write the same metre with very different results; the blank verse of Milton is on the whole easily distinguishable from that of Wordsworth's, and both of these from Tennyson's.

Romance is a narrative of adventure. In its prose form it differs from the **novel** as dealing little with ordinary life; its personages are royal or knightly, its events are marvellous. Love is an important element. Such tales must have been always popular, and the Middle Ages were devoted to them; but as they are not a part of classical literature either in fact or in spirit, they fell into disfavour at the Revival of Learning. Montaigne never knew such time-consuming and wit-besotting trash of books as King Arthur, Launcelot du Lake, Amadis, and Huon of Bordeaux; give him Ovid. To Roger Ascham they are " books of feigned chivalry, wherein a man by reading should be led to none other end but only to manslaughter and bawdry." Cervantes' attitude to romance in *Don Quixote* is the same. Scott is the great reviver of the romance in verse and in prose, but the marvellous element has almost disappeared, and the presentation of ordinary life has come in. Meredith's *The Shaving of Shagpat* is a quite unique modern imitation of the oriental tales which contributed to making the romances of the Middle Ages.

Romantic in literature describes the qualities characteristic of the romance, and is opposed to **classical.** The distinction is not easy to define. Exuberance, variety, splendour, a certain carelessness as to arrangement, interest in details—these are the chief marks of the romance, and they belong more or less to the great writers who led the romantic revival at the very beginning of the nineteenth century. Pater says that in the romantic spirit curiosity overbalances the desire of beauty ; it adds strangeness to beauty. It certainly finds the classical ideal of impersonal, abstract beauty less warm and interesting. But it is easy to find romantic elements in the great classicists, and *vice versa*.

S

Sarcasm is witty abuse; it is meant to injure what it is aimed at. When Mr. A.'s vanity was excused as being only skin-deep, the sarcastic reply was, "A very thick skin!" When **irony** is used with unkind intention it may amount to sarcasm; but it is often misunderstood. Pope's character of Addison is a famous example of sustained sarcasm.

Satanic School is a phrase invented by Southey with special reference to Byron's poems. "The school which they have set up may properly be called the Satanic School; for though their productions breathe the spirit of Belial in their lascivious parts, and the spirit of Moloch in those loathsome images of atrocities and horrors which they delight to represent, they are more especially characterized by a Satanic spirit of pride and audacious impiety, which still betrays the wretched spirit of hopelessness wherewith it is allied" (Preface to *The Vision of Judgement*, 1821). This is "calling names" with a vengeance, but Byron was even better at that form of sport.

SATIRE

Satire is a witty attack on some idea, institution, class or individual, and may be in prose or verse. The *Letters of Junius* are a sustained satire on the Government; in *Gulliver's Travels* Swift satirizes mankind in general, monarchs and men of science in particular. *Don Quixote* satirizes the idea of chivalry, but it is an almost unique satire, for its pathos is to many readers its predominant quality. Swift's satire is the product of a genuine indignation with all the pettiness and wrong of life. All satirists pretend to this indignation, but it is obvious that many of them find an artistic pleasure in the portrayal of the vices which they attack. " No great satirist would like society to be perfect," said Charlotte Brontë, speaking of Thackeray; and Tennyson held that—

> He never had a kindly heart,
> Nor ever cared to better his own kind,
> Who first wrote satire, with no pity in it.

But there is plenty of disguised pity in Thackeray's. Satire may take the dramatic form. In *The Doctor's Dilemma* Mr. Bernard Shaw satirizes the medical profession as Molière had done before him. Of personal satires the most famous are Dryden's *Absalom and Achitophel*, and the portraits in Pope's satires. Satire is always one-sided, and cares more for effect than for truth ; though a good satirist knows that a pretence of fairness will make his attack more effective. The satirist, says Coleridge, "takes for granted the existence of a character that never did and never can exist, and then employs his wit, and surprises and amuses his readers, in analysing its incompatibilities." Worse than this, he may commit " most mischievous foul sin in chiding sin." " When vice is led forth to be sacrificed at the shrine of virtue," says Warton, " the victim should not be too richly dressed."

Scansion.—By scanning a line we mean separating and naming the feet of which it is composed. When we have scanned a sufficient number of lines in a poem, we have shown clearly its metrical structure, and we have also done a good deal towards showing how exactly the **rhythm** is varied. But as rhythm depends not only on **accent** but also on **quantity** and **pause,** the scansion will not give a full account of it. A practised ear will readily perceive the **metre,** i.e. the normal line or lines to which all the others more or less conform, without scanning. This may be called the mechanical basis of the verse. But its life and charm come from the subtle variations of rhythm, and whatever mode of scansion we adopt, some of these will elude tabulation. However, the method here recommended enables us to compare, in some respects, if not in all, the rhythm of lines metrically identical. Here is a specimen, from *Paradise Lost*:

> His spéar—|to é|qual whích|the táll|est pine
> Héwn on|Nórwé|gian hílls,|to be|the mást
> Of sóme|gréat ám|miral,|were bút|a wánd—
> He wálked|with, to|suppórt|uneá|sy stéps
> Over|the búrn|ing márl,|nót líke|thóse stéps
> On héa|ven's á|zure ; and|the tór|rid clíme
> Smóte on|him sóre|besíde,|vaúlted|with fíre.

The first line is normal—five iambs; the second runs—trochee, spondee, iamb, pyrrhic, iamb; the third—iamb, spondee, pyrrhic, iamb, iamb; and so on. Notice how the light pyrrhic is sometimes compensated by the heavy spondee, and the pause which accompanies each. The initial trochees are very common in iambic verse; the trochee in the fourth foot of the last line is exceptional, and gives a fine rhythm. When a trisyllabic foot occurs, we accept it readily enough as a variation, but most of the eighteenth century authorities shunned it. As the number of accents in a heroic line varies between about eight and three, the number of syllables was taken as the basis, and that must be ten, or in the case of a feminine ending, eleven; so there was no room, on that view, for a trisyllabic foot. Our expectation of uniformity seems really to be divided between ten syllables and five accents; and it is hardly possible, perhaps, to give a rational account of the principles on which English verse is constructed. If we try to take account of weaker and stronger accents, we shall find much difference of opinion. Pronunciation varies a good deal, and so probably do the constructive principles of different metres. Here we have ventured only to deal with the standard English line, known as heroic.

Sigmatism.—English had a bad name for its profusion of sibilant sounds, "the hissing so much noticed by foreigners," says Addison. Tennyson was careful to write as few as possible; the process of exclusion he called "kicking the geese out of the boat," and he followed Quintilian's advice against the collision of s sounds : *si binæ colliduntur, stridor est, ut ars studiorum.* But Milton was less sensitive : e.g. on sands and shores and desert wildernesses: and seat of Salmanassar whose success. Coleridge, a great master of musical verse, actually quotes *Lycidas* thus:

<blockquote>
We had been reared upon the self-same hills,
Fed the same flocks by fountains, shades, and rills—
</blockquote>

where in Milton all the nouns are singular. Waller, whose name is proverbial for smoothness and euphony, could write "to whom soft sleep seems more secure and sweet"; and Rossetti has the line " whose kiss seems still the first ; whose summoning eyes."

Simile is a comparison stated as such, **metaphor** an implied comparison. Similes are common in ordinary speech : e.g. as clear as a bell ; as fast as the wind ; as cool as a cucumber. E. FitzGerald tells of a sailor describing a great storm : " And in a moment, all as calm as a clock." In oratory and poetry they serve to illustrate what is being described; they may only add clearness, but fine similes add richness or nobility ; independently of their complete correspondence in detail, they foster a state of mind in harmony with the main subject. This is perhaps a sufficient reply to the ancient reproach that no simile ever ran on all fours. Macaulay notices that whereas Dante's similes are the illustrations of a traveller, for clearness, not for beauty, Milton's suggest rather than describe : e.g. his Satan is a Titan or a sea-monster, Teneriffe or Atlas ; but Dante's Nimrod has a face as long and broad as the ball of St. Peter's, and his stature is that of three tall Germans. The famous comparison of Satan flying to a fleet far off at sea illustrates what has just been said ; Tennyson's comment is, " Was ever simile so vast as this ? " Jeremy Taylor's ornate prose abounds in similes beginning

SIMILE—SLANG

"So have I seen. . . ." This may degenerate into a trick, which will account for the king's indignation in Fielding's *Tom Thumb* :

> Curst be the man who first a simile made !
> Curst every bard who writes—So have I seen ! . . .
> The devil is happy, that the whole creation
> Can furnish out no simile to his fortune.

Cowper, bewailing the hard labour involved in translating Homer, has an agreeable parody of the Homeric simile : " As when an ass, being harnessed with ropes to a sand-cart, drags with hanging ears his heavy burden, neither filling the long-echoing streets with his harmonious bray, nor, throwing up his heels behind, frolicsome and airy, as asses less engaged are won't to do : so I, etc." There are many similar parodies in Fielding's novels. Arnold's *Sohrab and Rustum*, supplies some serious examples of the same imitation. On the Homeric similes there is an interesting discussion in Jebb's *Homer*.

Slang is a general term of abuse for current forms of expression which have not yet been received as standard English. The word " mob " was once odious slang. It often arises from an unconscious feeling that existing forms are tame, not sufficiently picturesque ; some genius invents a more coloured equivalent ; it is seen to supply a long felt want, and fashion does the rest. There is a certain knowingness implied in the use of current slang, a sort of freemasonry among those who use it. Being usually the invention of the less educated, it is liable to faults of taste; it often takes the form of violent metaphors, e.g. to kick the bucket, or stupid periphrases and metonymies; but perhaps its worst form is the misapplication of good words, which thereby cease to be available in their proper sense. It is almost impossible now to speak of a bloody war or an awful sight. This loss of definiteness in the meaning of a word is a common process in language. The word " nice " now is merely a vague expression of approbation. Indeed slang is a sign that a language is alive. Most of its inventions perish, but the fittest—those which really enrich our speech—may become part of the literary language, and survive. An odd piece of classical slang is the word " tandem," the Latin for " at length." The genius who first applied it to horses harnessed lengthways, not side by side, is unknown, but he was in his way a benefactor. The slang of different trades and callings sometimes contributes to the common stock: e.g. to strike oil. Specimens of university slang are " coach " and " grinder " for a private tutor. " Tuck " and " grub " are significant school slang.

SOLECISM

Solecism is properly "misusing the grammatical rules to be observed in genders, cases, tenses, and such-like . . . the breaking of Priscian's head, for he was among the Latins a principal grammarian" (Puttenham). But it also means any use of words not recognized by good writers. There is a treble solecism in "I shall be very pleased to accept your kind invite," for (1) as the acceptance is not in the future, the present tense is needed; (2) "very" should not be used with past participles; (3) "invite" is not a recognized equivalent for "invitation." It follows that solecisms are almost non-existent in poetry. Byron was careless, and could write "There let him lay!" meaning "lie," for the sake of the rhyme. A solecism which occurs in almost all writers, and cannot always be ascribed to the printer, is such a phrase as "one of the fastest boats that *has* ever been seen on the river." The older writers often used the phrase "the best of all others," a mixture of "best of all," and "better than all others." So "seldom or ever" is a foolish mixture of "seldom if ever" and "seldom or never." The so-called split infinitive, e.g. to nobly dare, occurs occasionally in good writers, e.g. Matthew Arnold, and some critics have been so bold as to justify it.

Sonnet is in form a poem of fourteen heroic lines, with a definite arrangement of rhymes. It has two main subdivisions: (A) that written by Shakespeare, three quatrains with six alternate rhyme-sounds followed by a rhymed couplet; (B) the Italian form written by Milton, the first eight lines or octave rhyming abba, abba, the remaining six or sestet rhyming more freely. In form A the final couplet, being somewhat sharply detached from the rest, is apt to take an epigrammatic point which affects the feeling of the whole. Form B tends to break the sense in two, the octave preparing for the culminating thought of the sestet, as in Keats on Chapman's Homer; but Milton often prevents this effect by running the sentence past the eighth line. The sonnet is thus a highly artificial form; it demands brevity, unity, the highest craftsmanship; and many critics, especially those of the eighteenth century, have thought it a mere conventional sort of trifling. Even Edward FitzGerald wrote of "little shapes in which a man may mould very mechanically any single thought which comes into his head, which thought is not lyrical enough in itself to exhale in a more lyrical manner." No doubt there are plenty of such sonnets, and even Wordsworth wrote some of them, but the Swiss painter Fuseli is more helpful: "If, as may reasonably be supposed, the first twister of a sonnet was a being of a versatile head and frozen heart, the beauties thronged into this little labyrinth, its glowing words and thoughts that burn, equally challenge our admiration and sympathy." Shakespeare, Milton, Wordsworth, Keats at his best, Mrs. Browning, and D. G. Rossetti showed what passion and loveliness may animate a seemingly rigid form. Its very difficulty may act as a stimulant; its brevity compels a naturally diffuse writer to waste no word; and to the expression of a passionate feeling it supplies the penetrating power of concentration.

Spenserian Stanza consists of eight heroic lines followed by an Alexandrine, the lines rhyming ab ab bc bc c. This interlacing of rhymes gives a binding effect, and the long closing line ends the stanza with great dignity. It was invented by Spenser for *The Faerie Queene*, " the only long poem that a lover of poetry can sincerely wish longer " (Saintsbury). The wonderful eighteenth century endeavoured imitation, but Shenstone's *Schoolmistress*—a charming humorous poem —and Thomson's *Castle of Indolence* are its only successes. In Shelley's *Revolt of Islam* the stanza soared again; indeed Swinburne says that Shelley gave " a more masculine force of music to that mellifluous form of metre—more of staying power to that overtrained Pegasus—than Spenser himself could give." He used it again in *Adonais*, the splendid Elegy on Keats. Keats's own *Eve of St. Agnes* is a noble success. Byron wrote some stanzas of considerable eloquence in the course of *Childe Harold*, but his touch is so different that one hardly recognizes the metre as Spenser's: and Campbell's *Gertrude of Wyoming* has been described as "the clumsiest caricature of the Spenserian stanza ever written by a man of real poetic power." Burns's *Cottar's Saturday Night* should also be mentioned.

Spondee is a foot of two accented syllables. It is a very valuable make-weight in iambic lines: e.g. Slow, slow,|fresh fount,|keep time| with my|salt tears (Ben Jonson). Milton has made splendid effects with a spondee in the last place: e.g. Silence, ye troubled waves, and thou deep, peace! The strong accent in English so lightens the unaccented syllables that spondaic words are very rare. Poe could find only " compound, context, footfall " and a few similar words. Hence our spondees must be made of monosyllables, or else be broken between two words. Swinburne in his sonnet on Shakespeare has achieved a completely spondaic line, slightly dis-

SPONDEE—STANZA

guised but certainly not shortened by two elisions:

> All joy, all glory, all sorrow, all strength, all mirth
> Are his.

Fairfax thus describes the effect on the crusading host of the first sight of Jerusalem: " Soft words, low speech, deep sobs, sweet sighs, salt tears."

Stanza is a combination or group of lines rhyming in a fixed order, repeated through a poem. The " verses " of hymns are a familiar example. The principal four-line stanzas are (1) **ballad metre**; (2) **elegiac**; (3) the *In Memoriam* stanza, previously written by Ben Jonson and others:

> Fair ship, that from the Italian shore
> Sailest the placid ocean-plains
> With my lost Arthur's loved remains,
> Spread thy full wings and waft him o'er.

(4) FitzGerald's stanza in *Omar Khayyám*:

> The Moving Finger writes; and, having writ,
> Moves on: nor all your Piety nor Wit
> Shall lure it back to cancel half a Line,
> Nor all your Tears wash out a Word of it.

Rhyme Royal, so called from James I, the poet-king of Scotland, is a stanza of seven heroic lines rhyming ab ab bcc. It is also known as " Troilus verse," from the fame of Chaucer's poem written in it, and was " the favourite stave of the fourteenth, fifteenth, and sixteenth centuries." Spenser's *Four Hymns*, Shakespeare's *Rape of Lucrece* and Milton's *The Passion* are written in this stanza.

The favourite Italian stanza known as **Ottava Rima** has eight heroic lines rhyming ab ab ab cc. Spenser's *Muiopotmos*, Fairfax's *Tasso*, Keats's *Isabella*, Shelley's *Witch of Atlas*, and Byron's *Don Juan* are some of the English poems written in it. Last comes the great **Spenserian stanza** of nine lines. **Terza Rima**, the metre of Dante's great poem, was used by Byron in *The Prophecy of Dante*, and by Shelley, especially in *The Triumph of Life*. It consists of groups of three heroic lines, the first and last of each group rhyming with the middle line of the previous group. It has been but little used in English; Sidney and Drummond have some specimens, and Milton translated Psalm ii. in it.

Stichomythia is dialogue of alternate lines, common in Greek tragedy, in Seneca's Latin imitations, and in the English writers who imitated him. Swinburne's *Atalanta in Calydon* supplies a modern example:

CHORUS. Yet one doth well being patient of the gods.
ALTHÆA. Yea, lest they smite us with some four-foot plague.

STICHOMYTHIA—STYLE

Cho. But when time spreads find out some herb for it.
Al. And with their healing herbs infect our blood.
Cho. What ails thee to be jealous of their ways?
Al. What if they give us poisonous drinks for food?

And so on. The complete absence of spontaneity in such battledore and shuttle-cock dialogue, as Lowell calls it, is quite foreign to the best dramatic writing in English. Sidney has a long dialogue between Reason and Passion, of which the following is perhaps a sufficient example:

R. Thou rebel vile, come, to thy master yield.
P. No, tyrant, no; mine, mine shall be the field.
R. Can Reason then a tyrant counted be?
P. If Reason will that Passions be not free.
R. But Reason will that Reason govern most.
P. And Passion will that Passion rule the roast.

Style is the form in which thought is expressed, the manner as distinguished from the matter. The distinction may seem obvious, and it is broadly just, for the same *sort* of thing may be said in different ways; but when examined closely it fails us. The thing said is not entirely independent of the way of saying it. For purposes of communication, at least, thought exists only in its expression. If differently expressed the thought would be, no matter how little, different. "Style," says Lord Chesterfield, "is the dress of thoughts." But there is no such thing as a naked thought in literature. Each writer will dress his thoughts after his own fashion, and it is the dressed thought with which we are to deal. Style puts us in touch with a personality; the famous aphorism tells us that "the style is the man." It follows that there are as many styles as there are writers, but certain broad distinctions are useful to observe. The most obvious is that between simple and ornate. Masters of the simple style are Bunyan, Defoe, Addison, Swift, Goldsmith, Southey, Wordsworth; of the ornate, Shakespeare, Jeremy Taylor, Milton, Johnson, Gibbon, Tennyson, Ruskin. And a writer may vary his style to suit his subject; contrast Wordsworth's *Lucy Gray* with his *Laodamia*. Abbott and Seeley roughly divide poetic style into (1) elevated, e.g. Milton, (2) graceful, e.g. Tennyson, (3) forcible, e.g. Pope, (4) simple, e.g. Wordsworth. A great virtue of style is ease; the reader must not be made conscious of the effort which has achieved simplicity, and again the ornate style must seem natural to the writer. Carlyle's strange language would be entirely unbearable if it did not impress us with its sincerity. Some writers, e.g. R. L. Stevenson, have acquired their style by long and laborious experiment;

STYLE—SYLLEPSIS

(to others it comes naturally); whereas Scott wrote his poetry twice, but his prose only once. Sometimes one can catch these deliberate stylists at work. Bishop Berkeley once wrote of Ischia in a letter to a friend: "As riches and honours have no footing here, the people are unacquainted with the vices that attend them; but in lieu thereof they have got an ugly habit of murdering one another for trifles." The same fact was told to Pope in this form: "The inhabitants of this delicious isle, as they are without riches and honours, so they are without the follies and vices that attend them; and were they but as much strangers to revenge as they are to avarice and ambition, they might in fact answer the poetical notions of the golden age. But they have got, as an alloy to their happiness, an ill habit of murdering one another on slight offences." But this is a playing with style. All true style, however acquired, is a product of personality.

Syllepsis is the use of the same word (verb or preposition) with different senses in the same sentence. The historian says of John Sobieski: "He flung his powerful frame into the saddle and his great soul into the cause." Sylvester's Moses asks permission for Israel to go to Horeb, that "their hearts and heifers they may offer there." Evelyn describes

Charles I as "circled with his royal diadem and the affections of his people." There is something comic in the incongruity of this double meaning, and it ought to be confined to light or comic style. Pope says of Sir Plume, the ambassador in *The Rape of the Lock*: "he first the snuff-box opened, then the case"; and in the Key, pretending that Prince Eugène was the person indicated, he says: "This general is a great taker of snuff, as well as towns." Cp. "he sat in a very clean shepherd's dress and a profound melancholy"; which recalls Dickens's "Miss Bolo went home in a flood of tears and a sedan chair." But Milton writes of "light-armed troops In coats of mail and military pride."

Synecdoche is that form of **metonymy** in which a part of a thing is put for a whole thing: e.g. keel or sail for ship, hand for a workman, soul for an individual whose death or conversion is contemplated. Cp. Byron's—

> He stood alone amidst his land,
> Without one trusted heart or hand—

i.e. one on whose affection or co-operation he could rely. A species of synecdoche is using the material for the thing made of it: e.g. the steel for the sword, glass for a drinking vessel. Bain also includes the use of a passion for the object that inspires it: e.g.

he is my aversion, my delight; the terror of the oppressor and the refuge of the oppressed.

Synonyms are properly words of the same meaning: e.g. begin, commence; humble, lowly. But, as Lord Chesterfield observes, "those who study a language attentively will find that there is no such thing." The usage of no two words is exactly the same. "Commence" is much less colloquial than "begin," and careful writers avoid using an infinitive after it. No one ever signed himself "your lowly servant." Hence the only practical use of "synonym" is to describe words of similar but not identical meaning. English is rich in such words, and their proper use is a difficulty to foreigners. "Shall" and "will" are an obvious example, and the distinction was doubly ignored in the famous cry "I will be drowned and nobody shall save me." "Ass" is more dignified than "donkey." "Hound" has come to mean a class of "dog." Scott has noticed in an often quoted passage of *Ivanhoe* that names of animals derived from French are now used for butcher's meat: e.g. pork, beef, mutton: the corresponding native words retaining their old sense. The Latin element has provided a number of alternatives: e.g. benevolence, good-will; fortitude, bravery;

apprehend, grasp; innocent, harmless. There is an unconscious economy exercised by the users of a language, in respect of such doublets; identical words are felt to involve waste, whereas differentiation of meaning or usage enriches the language. Dr. Johnson seems to have believed in the existence of synonyms in the full sense. He says that originally there were none, "but by using words negligently, or in poetry, one word comes to be confounded with another." Negligence will confound anything, and the poets of the eighteenth century really seem to have regarded such pairs as horse and steed, water and tide, nymph and lady, as practically synonymous. Johnson was misled by the practice of his day, a practice reformed by Wordsworth and the **romantics**; and we have seen that the general tendency of language is rather to discriminate than to confound. The use of synonyms to avoid the repetition of a word is a piece of modern delicacy, and should be avoided. It is painful to read such a sentence as this: "Eighty-three volumes are required for letter M, seventy-seven are demanded by L, and seventy-six are perforce conceded to B." Sincerity and good style demand the same word for the same notion, and skill can always avoid unpleasant monotony.

T

Taste may mean simply liking; we say that a man has good or bad taste according as he likes things artistically good or bad. But it is often used for good taste, which FitzGerald called "the feminine of genius," and Wordsworth the "refined co-mate of Truth and Beauty"; and Gibbon considered its purest source a benevolent heart. It may be a more charming, and is certainly a less constructive, faculty than genius, and therefore "feminine"; it is impossible without sympathy, and that is also the basis of benevolence, hence Gibbon's saying; but it is very confusing to put it on a level with Truth and Beauty, for it is in the perception of those great qualities that it exists. Carlyle is more helpful. "Taste," he says, "if it mean anything but a paltry connoisseurship, must mean a general susceptibility to truth and nobleness; a sense to discern and a heart to love and reverence, all beauty, order, goodness, wheresoever or in whatsoever forms and accompaniments they are to be found." It implies "a finely gifted mind, purified into harmony with itself, into keenness and justness of vision; above all, kindled into love and generous admiration." Many clever people are averse to this process of purification; they think their vision sufficiently keen and just without so much effort. "I know what I like," is their attitude, and they feel that submission to authority in such things savours of the insincere. But no skill worth having can be got without effort; and if we may without suspicion of insincerity improve our muscles, submitting to certain exercises provided for us, may we not blamelessly improve our judgment also? "Good taste," says Coleridge, "must be acquired, and like all other good things is the result of thought and the submissive study of the best models." But it is better to have no taste at all, than to pretend admiration for what we do not honestly admire.

Technical Terms are words and phrases which apply to some particular art or science. The propriety of their admission to poetry has been much discussed. Dryden in the preface to *Annus Mirabilis* claimed full liberty to use them; here is a stanza describing repairs after a naval action—

> So here some pick out bullets from the side,
>   Some drive old oakum through each seam and rift;
> Their left hand does the caulking-iron guide,
>   The rattling mallet with the right they lift.

We who are accustomed to Mr. Kipling find such technicality quite moderate, but it jarred against the eighteenth-century taste for the **general**; Pope blames Dryden for his "tarpaulin phrase." Addison, who truly admired Milton, censured his use of such words as pilaster, cornice, architrave, ecliptic, eccentric, zenith. But they belong to **rhetoric** if not to pure poetry, and the classical poets were not so squeamish as our Augustans; Virgil's *Georgics* abound in them. Dante at the beginning of Canto xxi of the *Inferno* has a detailed simile from ship-building, but, as Voltaire lamented, French taste forbade the use in poetry of the names of common articles, until Victor Hugo and the romantics gained their freedom; *Othello* was translated and acted; the provocative word *mouchoir* came, was heard with indignation, and finally conquered. Even in France such delicacy had not always reigned. Ronsard recommended poets to consort with men of all trades, so as to derive live comparisons from the terms of those trades. Scott notices Campbell as "the only English poet who has ventured upon the appropriate terms of modern fortification"; of course there is plenty of the old sort in Scott himself.

Transferred Epithet is an adjective used with a noun to which it does not properly apply, and belonging really to another noun often not expressed: e.g. "breakfast—that peevish, pale, that lounging, yawning, most ungenial meal," where the epithets really describe the breakfasters. Cp. a stationary voice, of a sentinel: seated over a pensive dish of tea (Goldsmith): old age, with its grey hair, and wrinkled legends of unworthy things (Shelley): Melissa shook her doubtful curls (Tennyson). In such phrases as Wordsworth's "the lowing mead," and Macaulay's "the shouting streets," the figure used is rather **metonymy**—mead for cows, streets for populace.

Tribrach is a rare foot of three unaccented syllables: e.g. protect us, there deci*phering as* we may: these crowded off*erings as* they hang: this straight-lined progress, fur*rowing a* flat lea: a damsel of high lin*eage, and* a brow. It will be noticed that in each case the first two syllables of the tribrach may by a rapid pronunciation be reduced to almost one.

Triplet.—Dryden varied the run of his heroic couplets by admitting freely groups of three rhyming lines, known as triplets. Pope seems to have doubted the **correctness** of the practice; his friend Swift made it one of his strictest rules in poetry to avoid writing triplets, "a custom introduced by laziness, continued by ignorance, and established by false taste." He never could resist having a hit at Dryden. Lord Orrery is heartily with Dryden in the great controversy. Johnson is uncomfortable about them; he approves of the variety which they introduce, but is worried because he can assign no rule for their introduction. Till such a rule is made he will tolerate their existence. Earlier than Dryden, Chapman affords a few examples, both in the fourteeners of his *Iliad* and the heroics of his *Odyssey*. Coming to modern times, we find that a triplet spoils the metre for Professor Saintsbury, " except in the very rare cases when its contents come in, in point of sense, as a kind of parenthesis or aside." So much for the triplet.

Trochee is a two-syllable foot accented on the first: e.g. weáry, gíve me. Jespersen notices how many ordinary phrases consist of two trochees: e.g. bread and butter: head and shoulders: rough and ready: high and mighty. Short trochaic lines are wearisome in quantity: e.g. Longfellow's *Hiawatha*. The trochaic line of $7\frac{1}{2}$ feet has been finely used by Tennyson in *Locksley Hall*. Tennyson varies the short trochaics of the *Ode on the Death of the Duke of Wellington*, by introducing an extra syllable at the beginning of some lines; and Milton, in *L'Allegro* and *Il Penseroso*, by dropping the first syllable of many of his octosyllabics, gives them a trochaic effect. In iambic verse, the trochee is a frequent substitute for the first foot, and is occasionally found in the others, very rarely in the last. See **Scansion.**

U

Unities, Dramatic.—This famous phrase embodies a theory as to the correct construction of a tragedy, which the French critics of the classical school wrongly believed to be Aristotle's. There are three unities, those of Time, Place, and Action. (1) The events exhibited must not have occupied more than twenty-four hours; (2) the scene must be the same throughout; (3) there must be only one main action, and under-plots, if they exist, must serve this main action. It is at once noticed that the great English tragedies take no account of the first two; even Greek tragedy, which had special reasons for observing them, did not always do so. The third "unity" is found in every great work of art, satisfying a fundamental desire of the mind. The French theory was popular in England in the days of Dryden; he treats it fully in the *Essay of Dramatic Poesy*, but he had too much good sense to accept it wholly.

Nobody accepts it now, though from time to time a writer will try his hand at writing a play within "the rules." Mr. Bernard Shaw's *Candida* is an interesting modern example.

W

Wardour-Street English is a phrase describing the inartistic use of **archaism.** It was invented in 1888, with reference to William Morris's translation of the *Odyssey*. Wardour Street had a bad name for the fabrication of furniture, etc., which falsely pretended to be old: in 1869 Swinburne wrote of " Wardour-Street armour "; hence the application to style.

Wit is a truly Protean word; seven senses have been enumerated in one poem of Pope's. Even its most ordinary sense is not easy to define. " It arises," says Coleridge, " in detecting the identity in dissimilar things," and all the critics agree with him. The detection of a merely verbal identity makes the pun, which has been described as the lowest form of wit, for it is the foundation of all. This is itself a witty remark, based on the double meaning of " low." If we consider wit as distinguished from **humour,** we notice that it resides in a certain form of expression, whereas humour belongs to a disposition of mind. Wit demands an audience; humour may be a purely private satisfaction. Humour is always kindly; wit either is sarcastic, or comes from a pure pleasure in the pointed expression of a thought. Sheridan was a witty writer, Goldsmith a humorous. Macaulay and Lamb may be similarly contrasted.

Barrow in one of his sermons has a celebrated passage on wit: "Sometimes it lieth in pat allusion to a known story, or in seasonable application of a trivial saying, or in forging an appropriate tale; sometimes it playeth in words and phrases, taking advantage from the ambiguity of their sense, or the affinity of their sound; sometimes it is wrapped in a dress of luminous expression; sometimes it lurketh under an odd similitude . . . sometimes it is couched in a bold scheme [figure] of speech: in a tart irony: in a lusty hyperbole: in a startling metaphor: in a plausible reconciliation of contradictions or in acute nonsense. . . . Oftener it consists in one knows not what, and springeth up one can hardly tell how."

Humour is frequently witty in its expression. An Irish lady, one of a festive crowd, being annoyed by the frequent and copious expectoration of a near neighbour, appealed to a policeman: "Constable," she said, "is it allowed to spit here?" And the guardian of the law and decency replied: "Eyah! spit away, miss!" The humorous misapprehension could not have been more neatly expressed. The late Colonel Saunderson aroused and calmed a dangerous storm of passion in the House of Commons, by calling an Irish priest a bloodthirsty ruffian and then substituting the words "excited politician." There was wit in the identification of dissimilar things; and there was great humour in the identification, considering the status of the speaker and his audience.

Z

Zeugma is a more violent form of syllepsis, using as part of two phrases a word which properly applies to only one: e.g. See Pan with flocks, with fruits Pomona crowned; however possible a crown of fruits may be, a crown of flocks is unheard of. The figure is very rare in English, but fairly common in Greek. In 1 *Timothy* iv. 3, " Forbidding to marry and *commanding* to abstain from meats," the italicized word is not in the original, but is necessary in English to give the sense.

TABLE OF REFERENCES

(The numbers in brackets refer to pages of this book)

ABBOTT AND SEELEY, *Engl. Less. for Engl. People*, 114 (18), 250 (90), 173 ff. (131), 132 (136), 69 (175)
ADDISON, *Spect.*, 35 (87), 61 (127), 135 (164), 160 (20), 285 (73), 297 (182), 512 (71), 573 (67), 619 (91)
ARMSTRONG, *A Day*, 60 (183)
ARNOLD, *Celt. Lit.*, 133 (153)
ASCHAM, *Toxoph.* (Arber), 19 (158)
AUSTEN, JANE, *Letter of* 1814 (40)

BACON, *Ess. of Truth* (141); *Adv. of Learning* (26)
BAIN, *Engl. Comp.*, 23 (177), 34 (41), 36 (27), 37 (28, 91), 42, 43 (141), 92 (134)
BENTLEY, *Serm. against Popery* (123)
BIBLE, *Job* xii. 2 (94), xxxviii. 31 (73); *Isa.*, xiv. 12 (85); *Luke* v. 14 (20), ix. 17 (70), xiii. 34 (28), xvi. 3 (38), xviii. 25 (88); *Acts* xxi. 39 (99); *Rom.* xii. 15 (70); 1 *Cor.* xv. 36 (124), 55 (28); *Col.* iii. 19 (85); *Rev.* v. 2 (89)
BIRRELL, *In the Name of the Bodleian*, 153 (25)
BOSWELL, *Johnson*, 1777 (105), 1779 (41), 1781 (20), 1783 (179)
BRIDGES, *Eros and Ps.*, March st. 10 (91); *on Keats* (93)
BROOKE, STOPFORD, *St. in Poetry*, 165 (20)
BROWNE, SIR T., *Rel. Med.* (Dent), 85 (11); *Pseud. Ep.*, ch. x. (20)
BROWNING, *Lost Leader* (50); *Hervé Riel* (154)

BURKE, *Reg. Peace* ad. fin. (21); *Subl. and Beaut.*, v. § 3 (36); *Corresp.*, ii. 347 (130)
BURNS, *Tam o' Shanter* (114)
BURTON, *Medinah and Mecca*, i. 8 (15)
BUTLER, *Hudibras*, I. iii. 617 (70), III. i. 791 (38)
BYRON, *Life*, 442, 711 (96); *Engl. Bards* (132),; *Hebr. Mel.* (21); *Ch. Har.*, iii. 24 (91), iv. 156 (123); *The Giaour* (177); *Beppo*, 44 (69); *Don Juan*, v. 8 (141), viii. 89 (123)

Cambridge Engl. Lit. (132, 171)
CARLISLE, LORD, *Sieges of Vienna*, ch. vii. (26), vi. (176)
CARLYLE, *State of Germ. Lit.* (180); *Richter*, i. (87)
CHAMBERLAYNE, *Pharonnida*, iv. 5 (122)
CHAPMAN, *Iliad*, pref. (142), viii. fin. (75)
CHAUCER, *Kt. Tale*, 881 (89)
CHESTERFIELD, LORD, *Letters*, 118 (174), 192 (178)
CHURCHILL, *Proph. of Fam.*, 135 (150)
CLEVELAND, *on E. King* (55, 88)
COLERIDGE, HARTLEY, *Essays*, ii. 1 (104), 117 (118); *Worthies of Yorks.*, 63 (44)
COLERIDGE, S. T., *Remains*, i. 90 (14, 71), 92 (16), 131 (188), 253 (162), ii. 172 (126), 107 (141); *Table Talk* (127); *Biogr. Lit.*, ch. 16, fin. (181); *Coleorton Letters*, i. 3 (96), ii. 164 (164); *Anc. Mar.*, 105 (155)
COWLEY, *Sleep* (107)

TABLE OF REFERENCES

Cowper, *The Task*, vi. 282 (64); *Letters*, Jan., 4, 1791 (147); Jan. 19, 1788 (166)
Daniell (Grosart), iv. 60 (12), 64 (58)
Darley, *Beaum. and Fl.*, introd., 46 (157)
Darwin, Erasmus, *Poems*, ii., 174 (57), 183 (137)
De Quincey, *Opium Eater* (91, 106); *Poetry of Pope* (16)
D'Israeli, *Cur. of Lit.* (52)
Donne, *Epigrams* (17)
Dowden, *Letters*, 383 (15); *Fragm. Lett.*, 161 (94); *St. in Lit.*, 242 (48); *French Lit.*, 381 (100)
Dryden, *on Lord Hastings*, 59 (43); *to Roscommon*, 59 (33); *Georgics*, i. 451 (19); *on Epic Poetry* (109, 128); *on Satire* (103, 107); *Ovid's Metam.*, dedic. (85), *Fables*, pref. (29, 44); *Mock Astrol.*, ii. 1 (49); *Rival Ladies*, pref. (92); *Alb. and Alban.*, pref. (147)
Dyer, *The Fleece*, iv. 249 (110)

Eliot, George, *Adam Bede*, init. (64)
Elton, Oliver, *Michael Drayton*, 100 (119)
Evelyn, *Diary*, April 11, 1640 (177)

Fairfax, *Tasso*, iii. 6 (172), viii. 78 (38)
FitzGerald, *Letters*, i. 87 (169), 225 (180), ii. 21 (165)
Fuller, *Ch. Hist.*, iii. 128 (134)
Fuseli, *Life*, i. 134 (169)

Garnett, *Ital. Lit.* (61)
Gay, *Trivia*, iii. 104 (145)
Gibbon, *Decl. and Fall* (Bohn), vi. 409 (127)
Gildersleeve, *Pindar, Pyth.*, ii. 48 (38)
Goethe, *Poetry and Truth* (Bohn), i. 231 (94)
Goldsmith, *Des. Vill.*, 222 (11); *Essays*, iii. (35); xvi. (79); *Cit. of World*, L (183)
Gosse, *Gray*, 114 (38)
Gray, *Progr. of Poesy*, 106 (13), *Elegy*, 33 (17), 63 (145); *Cat and Gold Fishes* (27); *On Viciss.* (38); *on Lydgate* (77)

Groos, *Play of Man*, 37 (15)

Hazlitt, *on Shakesp. and Milton* (126); *on Cowper and Thomson* (130); *Plain Speaker*, ii. 89 (116)
Henry, *Æneidea*, i. 206 (19)
Hunt, Leigh, *What is Poetry?* (40, 130); *Wit and Humour* (101); *on Eve of St. Agnes* (45)

Johnson, *Van. of H. Wishes*, 113 (64), 362 (145); *Cowley* (70); *Pope* (84); *Rasselas*, ch. x. (77)
Jonson, *The Musical Strife* (145)

Keats, *Ep. to C. C. Clarke*, 58 (14); *Endym.*, i. 229 (27); *Ode on Melancholy* (132); *Isabella*, st. 27 (146)

Lamb, *Letter*, July 1, 1796 (49)
Lewes, *Inner Life of Art* (157)
Lyly, *Euphues* (Arber), 43 (69)
Lytton, Bulwer, *New Timon* (133)

Macrobius, vi. i. 5 (139)
Meredith, *Trag. Com.*, ix. (124), xi. (35); *Vittoria*, xx. (115); *Love in the Valley* (121)
Milton, *Hymn Nat.*, 110 (41); *L'All.*, 25 (155); *Comus*, 209 (164); *Son.* ix. (155); *Par. Lost*, i. 27 (146), 293 (163), 359 (34), ii. 634 (165), 719 (88), iii. 1 (28, 56), 44 (34), 142 (37), iv. 408 (18), 604 (137), 721 (20), 740 (135), 848 (57), v. 195 (122), vi. 335 (91), 767 (153), vii. 216 (171), 433 (132), 503 (46), x. 346 (82), xi. 491 (38); *Par. Reg.*, i. 302 (14), iii. 278 (164), 311 (177); *Sam. Ag.*, 270 (150), *Eikonokl.* (139); *Hist. of Engl.* (91)
Morley, Lord, *on Aphorisms* (25)

Newman, *on Literature*, § 5 (136)

Orrery, Lord, *on Swift*, 225 (136), 297 (183)

Philostratus, *Vit. Ap.*, viii. 7 (87)
Poe, *Rationale of Verse* (49, 84); *Marginalia*, 139 (117)

TABLE OF REFERENCES

POPE, *Windsor Forest*, 37 (38);
Ess. on Crit., 345-7 (86, 109);
Rape of Lock, pref. (102), i. 17
(89), 36 (145), iv. 126 (177);
Ess. on Man, i. 77 (58), 96 (77),
iii. 221 (63); *Ep. to Cobham*, 95
(16); *to Murray*, 48 (22); *to
Burlington*, 150 (67); *to a Lady*,
55 (99); *to Arbuthnot*, 323 (24);
Epil. Sat., ii. 85 (30); *Dunciad*,
i. 90 (92); *Letter*, May 4, 1714
(36); Oct. 28, 1710 (182); *on
the Bathos*, ch. viii. (19, 33), xi.
(35), xiii. (74)
PRAED, *School and Schoolfellows*
(17)
PRIOR, *Solomon*, pref. (58), i. (20)
PUTTENHAM (Arber), 29 (97), 88
(37), 96 (52), 188 (82), 258 (168),
264 (140)

QUARLES, *Emblems*, iii. 9 (43)
QUINTILIAN, *Inst. Or.*, i. 5 (73,
142), viii. 6 (63), ix. 4 (164)

RABELAIS, ii. ch. 6 (102)
RICHARDSON, *Clarissa*, iii. 28 (38)
ROSCOMMON, LORD, *Transl. Verse*
(143)
ROSSETTI, *House of Life*, xxvi.
(165)
RUSKIN, *Mod. Painters*, iv. 12
(130)

SACKVILLE, *Induc. Mir. Mag.*, st.
42 (38)
SAINTSBURY, *Dryden*, 173 (184)
SCHOPENHAUER, *on Education*
(116)
SCOTT, *Life of Swift*, 433 (154);
Paul's Lett., 18 (182)
SELDEN, *Table Talk* (Arber), 95
(153)
SEWARD, ANNA, *Life of Darwin*,
187 (127)
SHAKESPEARE, *Rich. II.*, ii. 1 (44),
K. John, iv. 2 (136); *A. Y. L.*,
ii. 7 (162); *Merch. of V.*, ii. 2
(67); *Jul. Cæs.*, i. 2 (67);
Ant. and Cl., iii. 10 (89);
Lover's Compl., 335 (58)
SHELLEY, *Dæmon of the World*,
552 (16); *Alastor*, 398 (146),
460 (73); *Rev. of Islam*, 955
(183); *on the Punishment of
Death* (51)
SHENSTONE, *Schoolmistress*, st.
29 (145); *Economy*, iii. 80
(137)

SHIRLEY, *The Changes* (63)
SIDNEY (Cambr. text), i. 229 (41)
SKELTON, *Boke of Colin Cloute* (53)
SPENSER, *Shep. Cal.*, pref. (29);
Jan., 42 (73); *Epithal.*, 123;
F. Queene, I., xi. st. 28 (46)
STEPHEN, LESLIE, *Eighteenth Century* (48); *Hours in a Lib.*, ii. 38
(87); *Pope*, 27 (23), 196 (45)
STERNE, *Tr. Shandy*, V. iii. (30)
SWINBURNE, *Poems and Ballads*,
i. 73 (16), 80 (21); *Essays and
Studies*, 122 (57), 155 (129)
SYLVESTER, *Du Bartas* (1621), 260
(127), 45 (150), 355 (176)

TAINE, *Engl. Lit.*, ii. 14 (156), 105
(134)
TENNYSON, *Life*, i. 167 (86), ii. 11
(133), 15 (15, 164), 73 (131), 231
(148), 519 (165); *Brook* (23);
Princess, prol. (135), iii. (183),
v. (121), vi. (81), vii. (122);
Ulysses (157); *Sea Dreams*
(161); *Morte d'Arthur* (143);
In Mem., vi. (16); *Charge of
Light Brigade* (50); *Gareth and
Lynette* (81, 157); *Lancelot and
Elaine* (122), *Merlin and Vivien*
(122, 131, 135)
THOMSON, *Summer*, 905 (11)
THOREAU, *Walden*, vii. (38)
TRENCH, *Sacr. Lat. Poetry*, 43
(154)

VIRGIL, *Georg.*, i. 330 (19), ii. 492
(56); *Æn.*, i. 135 (27), ii. 353
(89)

WALLER, *Death of L. Protector*
(22); *Miscell.*, i. 35 (164)
WARTON, *Hist. Engl. Poetry*, § 65
(162)
WATTS, *Horæ Lyricæ*, pref. (103)
WHITE, GILBERT, *Letter*, Nov. 3,
1774 (59)
WITHER, *on Lady Scott* (46)
WORDSWORTH, *A Character* (24);
to Milton (28); *Solitary Reaper*
(64, 119); *Yarrow Unvisited*
(64); *Ode* 1816 (111); *Eccles.
Son.*, xvi. (154); *Why should
the earth* (180); *Excurs.*, ii. 750
(151); *Prel.*, vi. 136 (151), vii.
708 (38); *on Epitaphs* (44, 88)

YOUNG, *Ep. to Pope* (45); *The
Foreign Address* (145); *Resignation*, ii. (16)

PRINTED IN GREAT BRITAIN
BY HAZELL, WATSON AND VINEY, LD.,
LONDON AND AYLESBURY.

LIBRARY USE ONLY
DOES NOT CIRCULATE